OPTIONS TRADING:

© **Copyright 2019 - All rights reserved.**

The content contained within this book may not be reproduced, duplicated or transmitted without direct written permission from the author or the publisher.

Under no circumstances will any blame or legal responsibility be held against the publisher, or author, for any damages, reparation, or monetary loss due to the information contained within this book. Either directly or indirectly.

Legal Notice:

This book is copyright protected. This book is only for personal use. You cannot amend, distribute, sell, use, quote or paraphrase any part, or the content within this book, without the consent of the author or publisher.

Disclaimer Notice:

Please note the information contained within this document is for educational and entertainment purposes only. All effort has been executed to present accurate, up to date, and reliable, complete information. No warranties of any kind are declared or implied. Readers acknowledge that the author is not engaging in the rendering of legal, financial, medical or professional advice. The content within this book has been derived from various sources. Please consult a licensed professional before attempting any techniques outlined in this book.

By reading this document, the reader agrees that under no circumstances is the author responsible for any losses, direct or indirect, which are incurred as a result of the use of information contained within this document, including, but not limited to, — errors, omissions, or inaccuracies.

Description

Introduction

Chapter 1 Top Reasons to Trade Options

Chapter 2 Ways to Trade

Chapter 3 Covered Calls

Chapter 4 A Step-By-Step Way to Sell Covered calls

Chapter 5 Volatility

Chapter 6 Technical Analysis

Chapter 7 Vertical Call Spreads

Chapter 8 Advanced Strategies and Techniques

Chapter 9 Make Binary Options Trading Simple Through a Broker

Chapter 10 Options Trading Risk Strategies

Chapter 11 Top Mistakes made by New Traders

Chapter 12 Tips for Success

Conclusion

Description

Options trading is such a unique yet valuable way of making money in the stock market. While there are some risks involved in the trade, these are normally limited, giving you a chance to make some good money from the trade. Adequate market research and knowing when to make a move will help you succeed in options trading. Brokers can also assist too since they can help you trade before you master the business.

Trading in options is a process. The more prepared you are, the better the experience. Of course, the starting point lies in to understand what options trading is. Options are an alternative strategy for Forex investors who do not wish to trade in underlying securities. The basics involve understanding how to purchase and sell calls and puts. This is what constitutes an options contract.

With basic information at hand, you are now ready to attempt your first trade. The power of options lies in their versatility. However, this versatility comes with a cost. If not handled carefully, the trade becomes riskier than stock. That is why you will come across many disclaimers advising you to only engage in options trading using risk capital. This book plays a vital role in helping you appreciate the principle of decaying time and how it applies to options trading. Without understanding how this principle works, any trade that you carry out will be surrounded by diverse risks and uncertainties.

While you can succeed in options trading without carrying out any technical analysis, it may be difficult for you to determine the duration, direction, and range of movement within the market. Since options are always subject to decay, any slight change in the values is very important. Understanding technical analysis indicators such as the RSI, IMI, and MFI can go a long way to ensure that you manage volatility, minimize risks, and close your trades with a profit. As a trader, you must always choose an indicator that complements your trading strategy and style.

This book gives a comprehensive guide on the following:

- Top Reasons to Trade Options
- Ways to Trade
- Covered Calls
- A Step-By-Step Way to Sell Covered calls
- Volatility

- Technical Analysis
- Vertical Call Spreads
- Advanced Strategies and Techniques
- Make Binary Options Trading Simple Through a Broker
- Options Trading Risk Strategies
- Top Mistakes made by New Traders
- Tips for Success... AND MORE!!!

Introduction

An option is an agreement to buy and/or sell some financial assets. We call this asset the underlying.

Options have an expiration date in the United States; the sale could occur on or before that date. There is a pre-arranged asset price.

It is called an option because the buyer of the contract has the option to proceed with the transaction, and is not obligated to do so. If the owner of the contract (the buyer) decides to go through with the transaction, they are said to be exercising their rights under the options contract. While the buyer has the option to do so or not, the other party to the agreement is legally obligated to the terms set out in the agreement. That means they must go ahead and buy or sell the underlying asset if the buyer exercises their rights.

On the stock market, an options contract represents shares of stock. Typically, one contract is for 100 shares. And so the contract gives the buyer the specific rights. If it is a call option, they can buy shares of a stock with a fixed price per share. Meanwhile, for a put option, they are able to sell shares of stock at the pre-arranged price. This is a key point, and it doesn't matter what the current share price is when the buyer decides to exercise their rights. The seller of the options contract is legally obligated to honor the terms of the contract. This means they must buy or sell the shares at the pre-agreed upon price no matter what.

Options also expire in a matter of days, weeks, months, and even years from the present date. It's important to know the expiration date of an option because that has a large influence on the price of the option. Options that only last for one week are called weeklies, while options that last one year or more are called LEAPS.

It's seldom the case that the option remains in force between the seller and the original buyer because options are traded on their own market like stocks. An option is likely to change hands multiple times as options traders seek to profit or avoid losses. Option prices will constantly be fluctuating.

Most options expiration are never exercised, but you need to be on guard about this if you are selling options because if the current owner of the option would benefit by purchasing or selling the shares, there is a risk that they will actually decide to exercise their rights. The risk of this is quite a bit higher than normally portrayed in internet discussions about the topic, where it's often noted that "most" options expire without being exercised.

All of this might sound a bit confusing at first, but as we go along the details will be clarified, and it will start to make sense. Let's begin by exploring the two major types of options.

Strike Price

The price that is pre-agreed upon for the sale is called the strike price. That will be the price per share if it's exercised. So, for example, you could have an options contract for Apple. If the strike price is $180 per share, even though the Apple is actually trading at some other value such as $201 per share, the $180 price would be used if the option was exercised. The strike price is arranged and agreed upon when the contract is written and for the lifetime of the option.

Call Options

A call option is an agreement that gives the buyer the option to purchase stocks. The benefit to the buyer is the agreement contains a pre-arranged price, which is called the strike price.

Remember that all options contracts are optional for the buyer, which is the buyer of a call option is not obligated to purchase the shares. Buying a call option is a long investment, which is you are bullish on the stock and hope to profit from a rise in the share price. This can be done in one of two ways. The first way is to simply purchase the shares at their strike price if the market price of the shares has risen above the strike price. That way, the buyer benefits from being able to purchase the stock on a reduced price after the price of the shares has risen, possibly substantially. Then either they can turn around and sell them at a profit on the stock market or they could be satisfied that they were able to buy stocks at a lower price.

The second, and far more common way to profit would be to trade the option, that is, sell it to another buyer for a profit. An options trader can do this because when share prices rise in comparison to the strike price, demand for that option rises, driving up the price for the option. This is how most traders earn money trading options. So you could buy an option for $100, and then sell it for $150 a few days later.

Premium

This is the fee that is paid to purchase an options contract. The party who writes the options contract receives a fee from the buyer to enter into the contract. This is called the premium. The seller keeps the premium no matter what happens. The premium is quoted as the price per share, but note that an options contract covers 100 shares of stock. So if the quoted price of an option is listed as $2, the actual price you have to pay in order to purchase it is $200 (or $2/share x 100 shares). Although this entitles you to control the shares of stock, you don't actually own them unless you exercise the option.

Why Sell Call Options?

You might ask why someone would sell a call option in the first place since they can end up having to sell shares of stock. The reason is that selling options is a way to generate monthly income. As we will see later, if you already own shares of stock, you can sell options contracts against them and earn money from the sale. Owners of shares of stock that do this are making a bet that they can sell the options contract and earn money without having to sell their shares, but if you decide to sell options contracts be aware that in some cases the right to buy the shares will be exercised. So while you will profit from the premium you earned from the sale of the options contract, you may be forced to sell your shares of stock.

Advanced options traders can sell options contracts without having to actually own the shares of stock. These are called naked options, and we will discuss this more advanced method later in the book. By "naked," we mean that the options contract is not backed by anything. The danger is that the owner of the option (the buyer) will exercise it.

In that case, the seller of the naked call will lose money, because they would have to buy the shares of stock at the market price, and then sell them to the owner of the options contract at the lower strike price. So they would lose the difference: (market price − strike price + premium paid per share) x 100 shares.

If the party who writes the options contract owns the share of stock, it's best to enter into this type of arrangement when you can set a high strike price. In other words, choose a price that is higher than the price you originally paid to obtain the shares. That way even though you might be forced to sell the shares, at least you will make a profit on the deal. However, you won't make as much profit as you could have had you sold the shares on the open market. We say that you missed out on the upside.

In the end, selling options contracts is a bet against the stock, in the sense that you don't think the share price is going to go as high as the buyer believes it will go. If it fails to do so, the option will reach the expiration date, and it will "expire worthless" because nobody would buy shares that were more expensive than the going rate.

Call options have this name because the originator of the options contract might have to sell the shares of stock that they own; in other words, the shares will be "called away."

Break Even Point for Call Options

If you are buying call options, it's a good idea to have the break-even price in mind. In this case, it would be the premium + strike price:

Call option break-even point = premium + strike price

Suppose the market price is $50 per share.

Then, if you buy an option for $1 with a strike price of $51, the break-even point is $51 + $1 = $52 a share. So in the event you exercise the option, the break-even price would be $52 a share, and you'd want the stock price to go higher than that in order to make a profit.

However, if you are only buying options in the hope of selling them as the price of the options contract rises with rising stock prices, then the break-even price isn't really relevant. In that case, you only want the price of the option to go higher than the premium you paid for it. If you bought an option for $1 a share, then if the option price goes above $1 a share, you have a chance to profit, depending on what your broker's commission structure is.

Example: Buying a Call Option

Let's say a particular stock is trading at $50 a share. You buy a $50 call option (the strike is $50) for the stock with 45 days left to expiration. The price of the put option is quoted at $1.41, which means to buy the option it cost you $1.41 x 100 shares = $141. At 30 days remaining until expiration, the price of the stock has risen to $55 a share. Under these conditions and everything else being equal, the price of the call option is now $5.07, so you can sell it for $5.07 x 100 = $507, earning a profit of $366, less any commissions.

If you really wanted to buy the shares, you have the option to purchase the stock from the originator of the call option for $50 x 100 = $5,000 (remember 100 shares), which would save you $500 off the price you'd pay on the open market. Since you had paid $141 to buy the options contract, your net savings would be $359.

If you wanted to, you could then turn around and sell on the open market. This means you could sell them at the market price of $55 a share, for $5,500, leaving a profit of $5,500 - $5,000 - $141 = $359.

This serves to illustrate why under these circumstances the option is unlikely to be exercised since that is slightly less profit than you'd get simply selling the option to someone else. Where that circumstance might change was if the option was about to expire and you couldn't find a buyer for the option. That would still leave you with the ability to exercise your rights under the options contract and buy the shares at the reduced price, and then you could sell them immediately to get the profit.

Why Buy Call Options?

If you aren't interested in buying the shares, the main reason to buy call options is to profit by selling the option at a later date so that you can profit from price moves in the underlying shares. As we saw from our example, the price moves can sometimes cause dramatic increases in the price of the option. It isn't often that a stock is going to move $5 one way or the other, however, even a $1 or $2 rise in stock price can have dramatic effects. Consider an option on a stock trading at $51 a share with a strike price of $50 and 30 days to expiration. You could buy that option for $1.77 a share (total price - $1.77 x 100 = $177). If the share price increased to $52 the following day, you could sell the option for $2.42 (total price $2.42 x 100 = $242), making a quick $65.

With a call option, the benefit comes when the share price is higher than the strike price.

Even when call options have strike prices that are above the share price, they can appreciate in value when the share price of the underlying stock increases. So this also provides opportunities to earn profits.

Here are some recent moves that stocks made that would have led to enormous profit margins for people holding call options contracts:

Between June 17, 2019, and June 18, 2019, Apple increased from $194 per share to $200 per share.

On June 3, 2019, AMD was trading for $27.40 a share. By June 6, 2019, it was $31.84 a share.

On June 6, 2019, Amazon closed at $1,754.63. By June 18, 2019, it was up to $1,914 a share.

Between May 31, 2019, and June 11, 2019, IBM went from $127 a share to $135 a share.

Of course, stocks are not always going up, and you have to study the market closely to find opportunities. The point is that these opportunities are out there.

Put Options

The second class of options is called a put option. Like any option, it has a strike price with an expiration date. But in this case, the buyer has the option to sell 100 shares of the underlying stock. The transaction would take place at the pre-arranged strike price before or during the expiration date of the option. These are called "puts," and this stems from the fact that the originator of the contract is forced to buy shares of stock, so the shares are "put to" the party who wrote the contract.

Put options can be used in different ways. One way to profit from put options is by essentially shorting the stock. So when you buy a put option, you are short, believing that the stock will decline in price. Put options allow the owner to sell shares above the ongoing price on the market. That means they increase in value when the stock market declines.

Imagine that you buy a put options contract at $2 a share, for a stock trading at $50 a share. We could set the strike price to $48.

If the share price dropped to $46 a share or lower, you could buy the shares on the open market and then sell them to the originator of the put option at $48 a share.

Many options traders never exercise options but instead rely on being able to sell them at a profit to other traders before they expire. In the case of a put, you are still essentially shorting the stock because the price of the option will rise as stock price drops. In this case, you wouldn't buy the shares to sell to the writer of the put option, and you'd simply sell the put on the options market at a price that was higher than what you paid for it.

Example: Buying a Put Option

Let's say a particular stock is trading at $50 a share. You buy a $50 put option for the stock with 45 days left to expiration. The market price of the put option is quoted at $1.39, which means to buy the option it cost you $1.39 x 100 shares = $139. At 30 days left until expiry, the price of the stock has dropped to $45 a share. The price of a put option is now $5.02, and so the total price you could get selling the put option would be $5.02 x 100 = $502, fewer commissions.

Just like with a call option, if you buy a put option, you can exercise your rights, which, in this case, means selling the stock at a higher price than it's trading for on the market. If you already owned the shares, then the put option actually saves you from having to eat too many losses. That is, as the owner of the options, you can use sell the stock at $50 a share, even though it is trading at $45 a share. But remember you'd lose the price you paid for the premium, and so your net would be $5 - $1.39 = $3.61.

Some people buy put options to protect their investments in large numbers of shares. Owning a put option and being able to sell someone your shares at a much higher price than they are trading for in the market in the event a stock has a major downturn can be reassuring.

Even for those not currently owning the stock, you could buy them at the reduced market price, that is currently $45 a share, and then exercise your rights and sell the shares to the originator of the options contract at the strike price of $50 a share.

Why Sell Put Options?

Suppose that the party who writes or is the writer of the option has to buy shares of stock at an inflated price. This is because the strike price would be higher than the market price if the option were to be exercised. So you might be wondering why anyone would enter into such a contract. Again, there is a bit of speculation going on here. In this case, the seller of the option is speculating that the price of the stock is going to remain above the strike price of the option before it expires. In that case, they can earn money from the premium, which is the fee they received for the option.

Also, unless the stock is in a catastrophic situation, it might not be such a bad deal having to buy the stock. If it goes up in price again, then you can either break even or possibly see the stock price go high enough so that you can earn a profit.

Put options can be "protected," meaning that you reserve enough cash in your brokerage account just in case you need to purchase the shares. Remember they would be sold at the strike price. For example, with a strike at $40, you'd have to have $4,000 in your account in order to sell a "protected" put.

On the other hand, with brokerage approval, you could sell a "naked" put. This is equivalent to selling a naked call, meaning that the options contract isn't backed by anything.

How Many Options Are Actually Exercised

The big rub in this is that the vast majority of options are never exercised. In fact, only 10% of options are exercised. The others expire worthlessly or are closed out. That means that people who write options contracts have good odds that they can make a monthly income selling either calls or puts. Since most options aren't exercised, many traders earn monthly incomes selling naked puts. But if a put option is exercised, you had better be able to come up with the cash in order to purchase the shares at the strike price.

Put options give you the opportunity to profit from drops in the share price. Any $1 move in share price can mean big pricing changes in options.

Between April 23, 2019, and April 25, 2019 SNAP declined from $11.99 a share to $10.79 a share.

Between May 3, 2019, and May 14, 2019, SPY dropped from $294 a share to $280 a share.

- On April 24, 2019, Intel was trading at $58.72 a share. By May 1, it was trading at $50.76.

Knowing When to Buy Puts and Calls

The trick, of course, is to know when the stock will rise, which means buy a call option, or if the stock declines, which means buy a put option.

Knowing how to make your trades isn't going to be something you're going to be successful at very often simply going off gut feelings. Instead, you're going to have to put some time into studying the companies you plan to invest in, just like you would if you were building a personal stock portfolio, but in this case, you're going to be more interested in short term news that can move the stock. That means you're going to be looking for upcoming earnings reports and what the expectations are. You'll want to pay attention to news about products the company has on the market or plans to release. One earnings report that failed to meet expectations can send stocks tumbling; on the other hand, if it exceeds expectations, the shares will rise dramatically in price. Any product recall or failure can send shares tumbling, the release of an exciting new product like a new model iPhone that wows critics can send shares skyrocketing.

You can't predict everything ahead of time so you can't expect to win on every single trade, but by studying company fundamentals and keeping up with financial news, you can make reasonable bets that make for more wins than losses on your trades.

Options Pricing

Don't confuse strike price with options pricing. You will see options listed by strike price, but the price for the option is listed for one share. Remember that the option is for 100 shares, so the price you have to pay for the option is the option price x 100.

For example, SPY is a fund that tracks the S & P 500. The current share price is $293.17 a share. Looking at options, we see that they are listed as calls or puts by strike price. So we see a $294 call expiring in 2 weeks, with a price of $3.23. This means that the price to buy one options contract would be $323. If we wanted to buy 5 options contracts, it would cost $3.23 x 100 x 5 = $1,615.

In The Money

In this case, the strike price of the option is positioned favorably, in comparison to the current share price of the stock on the market. Call options are in the money when the strike price is below the trading price of the stock. For example, IBM is currently trading at $139.20 a share. That means a call option that has a strike price of $137 would be "in the money."

We say it's in the money because someone would benefit by owning the call option, because they would have the ability to exercise the option and therefore buy shares of IBM at $137 a share, which is cheaper than the $139.20 per share they would have to pay simply buying the shares on the market. In the money call options are worth considerably more than those options that are not in the money. For example, a $137 option on IBM option would cost a total of $377, while an IBM option with a strike price of $142 would cost $97.

Put options are in the money when the strike is higher than the market price. In that case, anyone who owns an option contract would benefit because they could sell shares of IBM at the strike price. Since they're higher than the price currently going on the market, they benefit.

In the money options always have a higher value. If the share price is $139.20, a $140 IBM put is in the money and costs $233. A $138 put option is not in the money, and so costs less, at $160.

At the Money

In this case, the share price is exactly equal to the strike price. You can buy at the money options as a strategy to save some money. This can be a good strategy because they may have a good probability of moving in the money in the coming days or weeks.

Out of the Money

In this case, for a call option, the market price is below the strike.

These options will be priced lower when compared to "in the money" options and "at the money" options. If there is a strong reason to believe that prices will move enough so it will be in the money at some point before the option expires since the prices are low, they can be a good bargain. But that depends on the specifics of market conditions and what's going on with the company at that particular time.

Now, consider puts. We say it's "out of the money" when it's market price is higher than its strike price.

When an option is out of the money, it can't be exercised, and so it's why they are cheaper. The main thing to remember about out of the money options is that they expire worthlessly.

To see how it works for a call, suppose the share price of some stock is $135 a share. Now consider is an option that has a strike price set to $140, for 100 shares. Then, if the share price remained constant:

At 30 days remaining, the price of a call option would be $71.

At 20 days remaining, the price of the option would be $41.

At 10 days remaining, the price of a call option would be $12.

With just five days left, the price of the call would be $2.

You can see that out of the money options rapidly lose value. This is because the pricing of the option when it's out of the money is tied up in the time value. Of course, if the price of the stock suddenly reversed, which it could in 5 days, this would turn into a profitable scenario. If the share price jumped to $140 3 days to expiration, then the option price would jump to $79. If later that afternoon it went to $141, then the price of the call option would jump to $139.

Of course, if you were to purchase an "out of the money" option close to expiration, you'd have to have good reason to believe the stock price was going up. Of course, if you were right, you'd probably be seeing some movement in the share price already because other traders would be bidding up the price. Also, it is unlikely you're going to have the kind of information the "smart money" or big institutional investors have before regular individual investors know what is going on.

Top Reasons to Trade Options

We've seen that trading options are an activity that has its upsides and its downsides. In this chapter, we are going to look at the top reasons that you want to trade options. Keep in mind that you can personalize your portfolio and investment strategy, so it's not necessary to go "all in" when it comes to trading options. You can have options trading as one part of a diverse investment strategy. In fact, many people use options to cover risks in other parts of their overall portfolio.

1. Trading Options provides an investment opportunity with limited capital

We then expanded on that and saw what kind of possibilities existed when investing larger amounts. However, if you are just starting out with investing, it's not necessary to buy more than one options contract at a time. You can invest for a relatively small amount of money depending on the stock. Trading doesn't have to be approached with an all or nothing mentality. You can start with small investments and work your way up by reinvesting your profits.

2. You can hedge your risks with index funds

Most people who invest in stocks will be investing in index funds in order to have a diversified portfolio. By utilizing options, you can hedge your risks with index funds. Index puts can help you mitigate losses if the market experiences a major downturn. Smart investors will utilize index puts so that the next recession doesn't leave them with huge losses.

3. Profit off of other losses

OK, it sounds bad when phrased that way. This is an opportunity that simply isn't available when doing regular stock trading.

4. Collect Premiums

This is another way to earn money in an overall investment portfolio that uses diverse strategies as well as diverse investments.

5. Capitalize on outsized gains

One of the biggest benefits that come with trading options is being able to control large amounts of stock that could have a huge upside if there is a major increase in stock price by purchasing a large number of call options. Of course, being a fortune teller isn't generally a lucrative income, but you can increase your chances of success by carefully studying the markets and the companies behind the individual stocks. Look for dynamic areas where new companies could see a huge gain in the stock price over a short period. The risk is that you'll lose your premium if the strike price isn't surpassed, but if it is then you'll have a chance to score big.

Ways to Trade

The main method for investing in the forex market, therefore, remains the classic forex market. When you operate on the forex market, you are actually buying and selling currencies.

However, over the years, other financial instruments have been introduced to invest in forex and currencies indices on the forex exchange. We are talking about CFD (contract for difference) and binary options. The main feature of these two financial instruments is the following: when you use them to invest in forex, you will not actually own the lots you are investing in.

That said, for those who do not intend to trading online, it could make little sense. Let's try to clarify. Both CFDs and binary options are contracts between investors and brokers. It's not like the classic forex market, where traders buy and sell among themselves. In CFDs and binary options, the asset movement (in this case the buying and selling of currencies) does not take place.

CFDs and binary options are used to speculate on the performance of the value of equity securities. If the trader's forecast is correct, the operation will lead to a profit; vice versa, if the trader's prediction is wrong, the operation will lead to a loss. So the mode of operation is similar to the stock market: if I invest on the upside, whether I do it with CFDs or actually buy currencies, I only earn money if the value increases.

As we explained in the previous paragraphs, CFDs are also derivative instruments, so they are used to speculate on the performance of asset values. This means that when you buy and sell CFDs, you will never own the asset traded (as opposed to classic forex trading).

Moreover, as with binary options, with CFDs it is possible to trade on:

- Equity securities
- Equity indices
- Forex currencies pairs
- Commodities
- ETF

Leverage plays an important role in CFD trading: through leverage, we can literally multiply the value of our investment. Just to give an example, if you use a lever of 1: 100 and invest € 100, thanks to this lever you can move well € 10,000 (using only your hundred!). All this is made possible thanks to the leverage, which is a sort of "loan" (if we can define it) by the broker, thanks to which you can invest more money than you really have.

But if we talk about eToro, we can't avoid talking about Social Trading. For those who do not know, eToro was the first broker to have introduced Social Trading in CFDs. Thanks to Social trading it is possible to invest by copying (automatically) the operations carried out by the other traders registered on the eToro platform. All you need is a couple of clicks to find the traders to follow, choose the amount to invest, and you're done. In this way, even novice traders can exploit the knowledge and experience of professional traders, copying their operations.

The online trading strategies are based on the study of mathematical and graphic analysis that can suggest the trader the best moment to buy and sell. As we have seen today, it is possible to invest in the stock market thanks to online trading, choosing between trading binary options and trading with the forex market.

Precise right away that there is no suitable trading strategy for all traders, but there are different trading strategies, based on traders and their style of trading. Therefore, it is possible to customize different online trading strategies on the basis of their trading objectives, their intellectual and psychological abilities.

We also recommend using 2 proven techniques not to turn winnings into losses:

stop loss: it establishes a maximum loss that you are willing to suffer;

take profit: you place a dynamic exit level that rises slowly.

Stocks vs. other investments

In this historical moment, the search for high returns has become almost spasmodic. Unfortunately, the expansionary policy of central banks has caused the collapse of yields (now virtually 0). Anyone who wants to get a positive return must take risks.

In this context, many are deciding to invest in stocks. What we are wondering with this chapter is whether it is really worth investing in stocks. The answer? It certainly is worth it, but it all depends on the modality of the investment.

This is an investment that can still guarantee very high performance, provided, however, to follow some guidelines.

The first tip is to use only really affordable platforms to invest in stocks. Among the best, we can definitely remember Plus500 or Markets. These platforms are characterized by the fact that they are very easy to use, even for those who have never worked with the actions but, at the same time, guarantee advanced tools, suitable even for the most experienced and needs. At the time of registration, you receive a free bonus that amounts to 7,000 euros for Plus500 and 4,000 euros for Markets. This is additional capital that can be used to operate on the stock markets but cannot be directly withdrawn. If you use the bonus and you get profits, these profits can instead be taken without problems and constraints.

Both Plus500 and Markets are Trading Contracts for Difference (CFD) trading platforms: this is a particularly flexible and easy-to-understand derivative instrument that guarantees the possibility of obtaining high profits both when markets rise, and markets fall. This is the second condition that makes it worthwhile to invest in stocks: if you buy shares directly, you earn only when the markets go up. And in today's financial conditions, it's an immense gamble. At this time, it is absolutely not convenient to buy shares, the thing that must be done is to subscribe derivatives (such as CFDs that are very simple) that have underlying actions. Plus500 and Markets are the ideal solution for investing in stocks and, incidentally, they also allow investing in forex, indices, commodities, bitcoins, etc.

If you want to invest in shares and you want to earn money, the advice is to open an account on Markets or Plus500.

The big advantage of stock investing: leverage

Through the use of financial leverage (or simply "leverage") a person has the possibility to buy or sell financial assets for an amount higher than the capital held and, consequently, to benefit from a higher potential return than that deriving from a direct investment in the underlying and, conversely, to expose yourself to the risk of very significant losses.

Let's see how the concept of leverage works starting from a simple case. Let's assume you have $ 100 available to invest Leverage financial in a stock. Let's assume that the gain or loss expectations are equal to 30%: if things go well, we will have $ 130. Otherwise, we will have $

70. This is a simple speculation in which we bet on a particular event.

In case we decide to risk more investing, in addition to our $ 100, also another $ 900 borrowed, then the investment would take a different articulation because we use a leverage of 10 to 1 (we invest $ 1000 having a capital initial only of 100). If things go well and the stock goes up 30%, we will receive $ 1300; we return the 900 borrowed with a gain of $ 300 on initial capital of 100. So we get a 300% profit with a stock that in he gave a 30% return. Obviously, on the $ 900 borrowed we will have to pay interest, but the general principle remains valid: the leverage allows to increase the possible gains.

Considering the further case of the investment in derivatives. Let's assume we buy a derivative that, within a month, gives the right to buy 100 grams of gold at a price set today of $ 5,000. We could physically buy the gold with an outlay of 5000 $ and keep it waiting for the price to rise and then sell it back. If we decide instead to use derivatives, we should not have $ 5,000, but only the capital needed to buy the derivative. Let's say that a bank sells for 100 $ the derivative that allows us to buy the same 100 grams of gold in a month to $ 5,000. If in a month the gold is worth 5,500, we can buy it and sell it immediately, realizing a gain of 500 $. With the 100 $ of the price of the derivative, we make a profit of $ 400, or 400%, at $ 100.

Without using derivatives and leverage, the same $500, I could have earned them only against an investment of $ 5,000, making a profit of 10%.

What are the potentials of its use?

The potential of leveraging is clear. But be careful: the leverage multiplier effect, described with the previous examples, works even if the investment goes wrong. For example, if we decide to invest $ 100 in our possession plus an additional sum of $ 900 borrowed, if the stock depreciated by 30%, we would remain with only $ 700 in hand; having to return the $ 900 borrowed plus interest and considering the $ 100 of our initial investment we would have a loss of over $ 300 on an initial capital of $ 100. As a percentage, the loss would, therefore, be 300% against a reduction in the value of the share of 30%.

Another element to keep in mind is that the different financial levers can be combined: in this way speculation operations are carried out using a "squared lever" with clear reflections on potential potentials.

What may appear to be an interesting tool with positive potential for the investor, on the other hand, presents risks that must, therefore, be taken into due consideration. In fact, if the financial system as a whole works with a very high leverage and financial institutions lend money to each other to multiply the possible profits, the loss of an individual investor can trigger a domino effect by infecting the entire financial market.

Banks are typically entities that operate with a more or less high degree of leverage: against a certain net capital, the total assets in which the resources are invested is generally much higher. For example, a bank with equity of $ 100 and leverage of 20 manages assets for $ 2,000. A loss of 1% of the assets entails the loss of 20% of the equity capital.

The development of the market for the transfer of credit risk (from financial intermediaries to the market) has meant that the traditional bank model, called "originate-and-hold" ("create and hold": the bank that provided the loan it remains in the balance sheet until maturity), has been substituted for many operators from the "originate-to-distribute" ("create and distribute": the intermediary selects the debtors, but then transfers the loan to others, recovering the liquidity and the regulatory capital previously committed or the pure credit risk (credit derivatives), with benefits only on capital requirements), with the effect of a further increase in leverage. The spread of this second bank model is one of the factors that explain the crisis triggered on the sub-prime mortgage market.

Covered Calls

In this chapter, we'll investigate a trading strategy that is a good way to get started selling options for beginners. This strategy is called covered calls. By covered, we mean that you've got an asset that you own that covers the potential sale of the underlying stocks. In other words, you already own the shares of stocks. Now, why would you want to write a call option on stocks you already own? The basis of this strategy is that you don't expect the stock price to move very much during the lifetime of the options contract, but you want to generate money over the short term in the form of premiums that you can collect. This can help you generate a short-term income stream; you must structure your calls carefully.

Setting up covered calls is relatively low risk and will help you get familiar with many of the aspects of options trading. While it's probably not going to make you rich overnight, it's a good way to learn the tools of the trade.

Covered Calls involve a long position

In order to create a covered call, you need to own at least 100 shares of stock in one underlying equity. When you create a call, you're going to be offering potential buyers a chance to buy these shares from you. Of course, the strategy is that you're only going to sell high, but your real goal is to get the income stream from the premium.

The premium is a one-time non-refundable fee. If a buyer purchases your call option and pays you the premium, that money is yours. No matter what happens after that, you've got that cash to keep. In the event that the stock doesn't reach the strike price, the contract will expire, and you can create a new call option on the same underlying shares. Of course, if the stock price does pass the strike price, the buyer of the contract will probably exercise their right to buy the shares. You will still earn money on the trade, but the risk is you're giving up the potential to earn as much money that could have been earned on the trade.

You write a covered call option that has a strike price of $67. Suppose that for some unforeseen reason the shares skyrocket to $90 a share. The buyer of your call option will be able to purchase the shares from you at $67. So, you've gained $2 a share. However, you've missed out on the chance to sell the shares at a profit of $35 a share. Instead, the investor who purchased the call option from you will turn around and sell the shares on the markets for the actual spot price and they will reap the benefits.

However, you really haven't lost anything. You have earned the premium plus sold your shares of stock for a modest profit.

That risk – that the stocks will rise to a price that is much higher than the strike price - always exists, but if you do your homework, you're going to be offering stocks that you don't expect to change much in price over the lifetime of your call. So, suppose instead that the price only rose to $68. The price exceeded the strike price so the buyer may exercise their option. In that case, you are still missing out on some profit that you could have had otherwise, but it's a small amount and we're not taking into account the premium.

In the event that the stock price doesn't exceed the strike price over the length of the contract, then you get to keep the premium and you get to keep the shares. The premium is yours to keep no matter what.

In reality, in most situations, a covered call is going to be a win-win situation for you.

Covered Calls are a Neutral Strategy

A covered call is known as a "neutral" strategy. Investors create covered calls for stocks in their portfolio where they only expect small moves over the lifetime of the contract. Moreover, investors will use covered calls on stocks that they expect to hold for the long term. It's a way to earn money on the stocks during a period in which the investor expects that the stock won't move much at price and so have no earning potential from selling.

An Example of a Covered Call

Let's say that you own 100 shares of Acme Communications. It's currently trading at $40 a share. Over the next several months, nobody is expecting the stock to move very much, but as an investor, you feel Acme Communications has solid long-term growth potential. To make a little bit of money, you sell a call option on Acme Communications with a strike price of $43. Suppose that the premium is $0.78 and that the call option lasts 3 months.

For 100 shares, you'll earn a total premium payment of $0.78 x 100 = $78. No matter what happens, you pocket the $78.

Now let's say that over the next three months the stock drops a bit in price so that it never comes close to the strike price, and at the end of the three-month period, it's trading at $39 a share.

The options contract will expire, and it's worthless. The buyer of the options contract ends up empty-handed. You have a win-win situation. You've earned the extra $78 per 100 shares, and you still own your shares at the end of the contract.

Now let's say that the stock does increase a bit in value. Over time, it jumps up to $42, and then to $42.75, but then drops down to $41.80 by the time the options contract expires. In this scenario, you're finding yourself in a much better position. In this case, the strike price of $43 was never reached, so the buyer of the call option is again left out in the cold. You, on the other hand, keep the premium of $78, and you still get to keep the shares of stock. This time since the shares have increased in value, you're a lot better off than you were before, so it's really a win-win situation for YOU, even though it's a losing situation for the poor soul who purchased your call.

Sadly, there is another possibility, that the stock price exceeds the strike price before the contract expires. In that case, you're required to sell the stock. You still end up in a position that isn't all that bad, however. You didn't lose any actual money, but you lost a potential profit. You still get the premium of $78, plus the earnings from the sale of the 100 shares at the strike price of $43.

A covered call is almost a zero-risk situation because you never actually lose money even though if the stock price soars, you obviously missed out on an opportunity. You can minimize that risk by choosing stocks you use for a covered call option carefully. For example, if you hold shares in a pharmaceutical company that is rumored to be announcing a cure for cancer in two months, you probably don't want to use those shares for a covered call. A company that has more long-term prospects but probably isn't going anywhere in the next few months is a better bet.

How to go about creating a covered call

To create a covered call, you'll need to own 100 shares of stock. While you don't want to risk a stock that is likely to take off in the near future, you don't want to pick a total dud either. There is always someone willing to buy something – at the right price. But you want to go with a decent stock so that you can earn a decent premium.

You start by getting online at your brokerage and looking up the stock online. When you look up stocks online, you'll be able to look at their "option chain" which will give you information from a table on premiums that are available for calls on this stock. You can see these listed under bid price. The bid price is given on a per share basis, but a call contract has 100 shares. If your bid price is $1.75, then the actual premium you're going to get is $1.75 x 100 = $175.

An important note is that the further out the expiration date, the higher the premium. A good rule of thumb is to pick an expiry that is between two and three months from the present date. Remember that the longer you go, the higher the risk because that increases the odds that the stock price will exceed the strike price and you'll end up having to sell the shares.

You have an option (no pun intended) with the premium you want to charge. Theoretically, you can set any price you want. Of course, that requires a buyer willing to pay that price for you to actually make the money. A more reasonable strategy is to look at prices people are currently requesting for call options on this stock. You can do this by checking the asking price for the call options on the stock. You can also see prices that buyers are currently offering by looking at the bid prices. For an instant sale, you can simply set your price to a bid price that is already out there. If you want to go a little bit higher, you can submit the order and then wait until someone comes along to buy your call option at the bid price.

To sell a covered call, you select "sell to open."

Benefits of Covered Calls

- A covered call is a relatively low-risk option. The worst-case scenario is that you'll be out of your shares but earn a small profit, a smaller profit than you could have made if you had not created the call contract and simply sold your shares. However, you also get the premium.
- A covered call allows you to generate income from your portfolio in the form of premiums.
- If you don't expect any price moves on the stock in the near term and you plan on holding it long term, it's a reasonable strategy to generate income without taking much risk.

Risks of Covered Calls

- Covered calls can be a risk if you're bullish on the stock, and your expectations are realized, and there is a price spike. In that case, you've traded the small amount of income of the premium with a voluntary cap of the strike price for the potential upside you could have had if you had simply held the stock and sold it at the high price.

- If the stock price plummets, while you still get the premium, the stocks will be worthless unless they rebound over the long term. You shouldn't use a call option on stocks that you expect to be on the path to a major drop in the coming months. In that case, rather than writing a covered call, you should simply sell the stocks and take your losses. Alternatively, you can continue holding the stocks to see if they rebound over the long term.

A Step-By-Step Way to Sell Covered calls

Now that you know about how important it is to sell covered calls, and how they can help you, let's take a moment to go through the different options and how you can sell covered calls effectively. Here, we'll take you through each of the steps, and why they matter.

Step One: Beginning with Choosing the Underlying Security

The first thing that you need to make sure that you have is, of course, the underlying security, which is what you're going to sell to investors in order to have them try to purchase for lower, or higher than what it is on the market. The call option essentially allows for the person to potentially buy it in the future. The seller would be the one with the options that don't get rid of them until the person decides to buy the stock.

First, you need to choose security that works for you. Look at the different stocks that you own and look to see the ones that have good dividends, that you're willing to keep for a while, but if you did sell them, there wouldn't be much love lost. You should, for example, choose 100 shares of a stock that you own, and you can see that the stock is getting close to the price that you'd sell it. One option does equal 100 shares, so you'd write a single covered call on the stock that you have. Of course, not all stocks have underlying options, and usually, the stocks with underlying options are ones with a higher value.

Step Two: Calculating Before Writing

Before you execute this trade, you should make sure that you always make sure that you do look at how much you're going to get from this. If you feel like this covered call should be done at a certain time period, you should wait.

When you're back here, you'll want to put into the covered call calculator the stock price, options price, and the number of shares, and you may need to add in commission fees and margins, and you should make sure that you choose for the options excised to be there, and you can calculate. You should also choose whether the option exercised is set to *no* to see the difference. You can also look to buy-write or overwrite the stock that you have, and the broker can also add some instructions onto these too. Do put your covered call through the calculator before you begin.

While the sheet is relatively easy to fill out on your brokerage site, this prevents a lot of issues from coming about, and can also give you a good idea of what you're going to do next.

Step Three: Heading to the Brokerage to Fill Out the Sheet

Next, you got to your brokerage and go to the options order entry form, which is where you look at the contract you're putting together, the limit price, the stop price, the transaction, order type, duration, and also the expiration date.

Next, remember that options expire every third Friday, so you should always make sure that you do this. Now, you should look at the stock itself, see what the strike price for this, and what you're willing to sell for, and the premium price on this. Let's say that if it does close higher, it will get exercised, so you lose the stock, but the thing is, you're still making money. But if it's lower, you get to keep the shares, and the premium, which means that it's literally just posting, having people purchase options, and then rinse and repeat.

Remember that one contract equals 100 shares of stock, so if you have 300 shares of stock, only do one at a time. The limit price and order type are also important to make sure that you have a limit there to prevent them from selling or falling to a different price.

There is also the transactions tab, which is where investors get confused. This is usually the "sell to open" option, which means that you're selling this to open the position. If you want to buy back the one that you sold, or buy long, you choose the option of buy to close.

You can then choose the duration, and how long it will stay, and you can also choose all-or-none with this, and you choose whether or not you can trade this. You can't usually choose the preferred ECN but leave it on auto.

Step Four: Watching the Market

At this point, you've got three options for well, your option and covered call, and they're important to note. The first is the stock goes down, so the call will be worthless, and you have to sell it for the price of the option. If you notice that it takes a dive before the expiration date, don't freak out. While there might be some losses, you'll notice that the stock itself goes down in value, so you can buy it back for less money than you got to sell it. If the option on the stock is changed, you close the position, buy back the call contract, and go from there.

So let's say that you have an options contract that's going for $100 and the strike price is $105. If the price goes all the way down to 20, you might have to sell the stock at that price if someone bought a contract for it, but if you still have the premium, you can then buy it again for that low price. You will have to sell if the option is exercised, but again, this is something that you can decide for yourself, and if someone buys a contract.

There is also the option that it stays the same or goes up but doesn't reach too high. This isn't that bad, because the call option will expire, so you pocket the premium, and you will still have the stock that you initially had. Not something that you can complain about.

Finally, you have scenario 3, and that is that the stock rises above what the strike price is. If this happens, then you're going to assign the call option to this stock, and that means you will be forced to share those 100 shares of stock. So, unfortunately, you still lose the stock. Most of the time though, since you're still netting a profit, there isn't as much love lost as you might think.

But, there is another issue that comes about with this. That is, if the stock skyrockets after you sell the shares, you're probably going to notice that you could've netted a huge profit from this. This is when a lot of investors tend to kick themselves for this, but the truth is, you shouldn't do that. This is actually a decision that you made when you chose to part with the stock at the strike price that you desired, and you still achieved profit from this.

That is the common problem a lot of investors face when it comes to selling stocks. They think that they shouldn't have done it just because the price for it skyrocketed to a whole different height. But, that's not always the case. You shouldn't feel down about this, and it can be a bit disheartening, but realize that you're not terrible for choosing the option to part with this. Sometimes, you may not even realize that the stock is going to fluctuate with time, and that is why, when you're choosing stocks for covered calls, they should be stocks that would very rarely have that much of a rise in price, and while having that volatility is good, you should also make sure that it isn't so volatile that you can't predict how it may go next.

When it comes to improving your covered calls, the best thing to do is to research and hold onto the stock. If you do have older stock that you just don't want to hold onto anymore, then I do suggest that you consider the option of writing covered calls on them. Remember, there are always times when you can buy these back too, so if you want to get the stock back and cash in on those dividends, it can be quite worth your while to do this.

Volatility

There's one final factor that affects the prices of contracts on a fundamental basis, though it's not really something we've touched on so far. The volatility of a contract is, however, an incredibly important concept to grasp for an options trader.

Volatility refers to the movement of the underlying stock. Some stocks will slowly wend their way up and down in a predictable manner – those are not very volatile. Others change on a day to day basis and change between up and down along the way.

To sum up the effect of volatility in a single sentence: the more volatile the stock, the more that an options trader is willing to pay for it. A volatile stock has a better chance of reaching the strike price and perhaps shooting far beyond it before the expiration date.

However, it's also the most dangerous of the factors that you need to bear in mind because it's arguably the most likely one to force you into a bad decision. A volatile stock, for example, can lead to a much higher premium and therefore a higher contract price; unless that stock shoots through the roof, you could actually end up losing money even when you should be making it.

One way to estimate the volatility of a stock is to take a look at what it has done in the recent past. This tells you how much it has moved up and down already, which some use as an indicator of how much it will move up and down in the future.

Unfortunately, it's not always true that the past repeats itself and you can't predict the future based on what's already happened. Instead, options traders use "implied volatility" to make their guesses: the value that the market believes the option is worth.

You can see this reflected in the activity on the options for that stock. Buyers will be keen to get their hands on options before a certain event takes place, such as the announcement of a new product or a release about the company's earnings. Because of this, options increase in price because there is implied volatility – the market thinks the stock is going to shoot up.

You'll see lower demand on a stock that's flat or moving gently, because there is no implied volatility and therefore no hurry to get in on the action. You'll also see correspondingly low prices for the option.

Volatility is obviously a good thing – as a buyer, you want the stock to be volatile, because you need it to climb to the strike price and beyond. However, there is also such a thing as too much volatility. It's at that point the contracts become popular, the prices rise and you stand to pay more for a contract than you will ultimately profit.

Your brokers will likely be able to provide you with a program that will help you determine implied volatility, asking you to enter certain factors and then calculating it for you. However, it's only through experience that you'll learn how to spot a stock that's just volatile enough to justify its higher price – again, practice is key.

It's also worth noting that a lot of the risk in options trading comes from volatility, largely because it's impossible to be accurate in your estimates. What happens if an earthquake destroys that company's headquarters? Stocks are going to plummet, and you had absolutely no way to see it coming.

That's why options traders are forced to accept that their fancy formulas are not going to be perfect predictors. They will help, but you should still be conservative in your trading and avoid the temptation to sink everything into a trade you believe could make your fortune thanks to its volatility.

Strategies for a Volatile Market

Long Straddle

This strategy is essentially an amalgamation of the long call and long put trading strategies. You will be using the money options for executing the strategy. You are required to purchase at the money calls along with at the money puts of the same amount. Execute both these transactions simultaneously and ensure that the expiry date for them stays the same. Given that the expiry date is long-term, it gives the underlying security sufficient time to show a price movement and increases your chances of earning a profit. A short-term expiration date doesn't provide much scope for any changes in the price of an asset, so the profitability is also relatively low.

Long Strangle

This is also known as the strangle strategy, and you must place simultaneous orders with your broker. You must purchase calls on relevant security and then by the same number of puts on the security. The options contracts you execute must be out of the money and must be made simultaneously. The best way to go about it is to purchase those securities that are just out of the money instead of ones which are far out of the money. Make sure that the strike prices in both these transactions are equidistant from the existing trading price of the underlying asset.

Strip Straddle

This strategy is quite similar to a long straddle- you will be purchasing at the money calls and at the money puts. The only difference is that the number of puts you purchase will be higher than the calls your purchase. The expiry date and the underlying asset for both these transactions you make will be the same. The only factor upon which your profitability lies on is the ratio of puts to calls you use. The best ratio is to purchase two puts for every call you make.

Strip Strangle

You stand to earn a profit if the underlying asset makes a big price movement in either direction is. However, your profitability increases if the price movement is downwards instead of upwards. You will be required to purchase out of the money calls and out of the money puts. Ensure that the number of out of the money puts you make are greater than the out of the money calls you to decide to make. So, to begin with, the ratio of 2:1 will work well for you.

Strap Straddle

This is quite similar to the long straddle strategy- you are required to purchase at the money calls along with at the money puts for the same date of expiry. You are required to purchase more calls than ports, and the basic ratio to start with is 2:1. User strategy for certain that there will be an upward movement in the price of the underlying asset instead of a downward price movement.

Strap Strangle

This is quite similar to the Long strangle strategy and uses it when you're quite confident that there will be a dramatic movement in the price of the underlying strategy. You tend to earn a profit if the price moves in either direction, but your profitability increases in the price movement are upward. There are two transactions you must execute- purchase out of the money puts and purchase out of the money calls options. However, the number of out of the money calls you to make must be greater than the out of the money puts. The ratio of out of the money puts out of the money calls must be two to one. So, you will essentially be purchasing twice as many calls as sports.

Long Gut

You are required to purchase in the money call options along with an equal number of in the money put options. All of these will be based on the same underlying security along with the same date of expiration. The decisions you are required to make while using the strategy are related to the strike price you want to use and the date of expiration. It is suggested that to increase your profitability, and reduce the upfront costs, the strike price you must opt for must be closely related to the current trading price of the underlying asset.

Call Ratio Back spread

You are required to purchase calls and right calls to create a call ratio back spread. Since it is a ratio spread, the number of options you execute in each of these transactions will not be the same. As a rule of thumb, try to purchase two calls for every call you write. Always ensure that the total credit for the contracts you've written must be higher than the total debit for the contracts you have acquired.

Put Ratio Back spread

You will earn a profit if the price of the underlying asset moves in either direction; however, your profitability increases if the price of the underlying asset's price goes down instead of going up. You are required to purchase puts and write puts simultaneously. As is obvious, both of these transactions will be based on the same underlying asset. The only difference is that instead of purchasing an equal number of puts, you will be purchasing to puts for every put you right. The puts you purchase must be at the money while the once you write must be in the money. The expiry date, along with the underlying security, must be the same.

Short Calendar Call Spread

The strategy is best used when you are certain that there will be a significant price movement in the value of the underlying security. However, you are uncertain of the direction in which the security will swing. Instead of spending a lot of time trying to analyze the direction of the price change, you can use the strategy. The strategy is likely complicated, and beginners must not attempt it in the first try. There are two transactions you must make. The first transaction is to purchase at the money calls, and the second transaction is to write at the money calls. Since it is a calendar spread, the expiry date is used for both these transactions must be different. The options you decide to purchase must be short-term with a relatively close expiry date while the options you write must be long term with a longer date of expiration.

Short Calendar Put Spread

There are two transactions that are required to execute in this strategy- purchase at the money puts while writing at the money puts. The date of expiration for both these transactions will be different since it is a calendar spread. The price of the contracts that have a longer expiry date will be quite high as compared to the ones with a shorter expiration date. It is based on the basic idea that a substantial movement in the value of the underlying security will mean that the extrinsic value of both the sets of options will end up being equal or close to being full. The initial credit you receive is because of the higher extrinsic value of the options written. So, if the extrinsic value becomes equal on both sites, then that credit which will be created is your profits.

Short Butterfly Spread

There are three transactions you are required to execute while using the strategy. You can either opt for calls or puts. However, for the purpose of illustration, let us consider using calls instead of puts. The principle used will stay the same. The first transaction you are required to make is sold in the money calls, then sell the same number of out of the money calls and finally purchase twice as many at the money calls. You are free to select varying dates of expiration, but it is a good idea to stick with the same date. The only major decision you required to make is related to the strike price. Ensure that the distance between the strike price and the current price is equal. It means that the in the money calls must be as in the money as the out of the money calls are out of the money.

Short Condor Spread

You are free to adjust the strike prices of the options you execute for optimizing your preferences of profitability along with the breakeven ranges. Only use this strategy after you gained some experience as an options trader. There are four transactions you required to execute in a short condor spread. You can use either calls or spreads, but in this example, we'll talk about using calls. Once again, the principle of execution stays the same regardless of it being a call or a put option. The first transaction you are required to execute is right deep in the money calls, and the second transaction is to purchase in the money calls at a higher strike price than the previous calls. The third transaction is to write far out of the money calls and then purchase out of the money calls at a lower strike price than the previous one. The number of options in each set of sale and purchase must be the same along with the date of expiration. The only decision you required to make is related to the strike price you use. The potential of your profitability depends on the strike price you use. The greater is the difference between the strikes and the current price; the higher is your potential to earn a profit. If this range of difference is high, then the strategy is known as a short albatross spread.

Reverse Iron Butterfly Spread

You are required to place for doors while executing the strategy. For the sake of simplicity, always execute these transactions simultaneously. You're required to purchase and write both calls as well as put options. Write out of the money calls, purchase at the money calls, write out of the money puts, and then purchase at the money puts. The number of options you execute while purchasing and buying the sets of calls or puts must be the same. Also, the expiration date must stay the same.

Reverse Iron Condor Spread

There are four transactions you are required to perform simultaneously to maximize your profitability while using this technique. You must purchase out of the money puts, then sell out of the money puts at a lower strike price stands the put in the previous transaction. You must purchase out of the money calls and then sell out of the money calls at a higher strike price than the ones used in the previous transaction. The number of contracts you purchase or write in each of the four transactions must be the same, along with their expiration date. The transactions very are selling the contracts; ensure that they are further out of the money than the transactions where you are purchasing the contracts. If the difference in these strike prices is quite significant, it is known as a reverse iron albatross spread.

Technical Analysis

Technical analysis is the method of using charts and other recording methods to analyze various data in options trading. Using these visual instruments, you have the chance to determine the direction of the market because they give you a trend.

This method focuses on studying the supply and demand of a market. The price will be seen to rise when the investor realizes the market is undervalued, and this leads to buying. If they think that the market is overvalued, the prices will start falling, and this is deemed the perfect time to sell.

You need to understand the movement of the various indicators to make the perfect decision. This method works on the premise that history usually repeats itself – a huge change in the prices affects the investors in any situation.

History

Technical analysis has been used over the years in trades. The technical analysis methods have been used for over a hundred years to come up with deductions regarding the market.

In Asia, the use of technical analysis led to the development of candlestick techniques, and it forms the main charting techniques.

Over time, more tools and techniques have come up to help traders come up with predictions of the prices in various markets.

There are many indicators that you can use to determine the direction of the market, but only a few are valuable to your course. Let us look at the various indicators and how to use them.

Support and Resistance

These levels occur at points where both the buyer and the seller aren't dormant. These levels are displayed on the chart using a horizontal line extended in the past to the future.

The different prices reach at the support and resistance points in the future.

How to Apply Support and Resistance

- Using these points allows you to know when to call or put.

- Support and resistance give you a way to determine the entry point to use for a directional trade.

The Significance of Trends in Option Trading

Technical analysis works on the premise of the trend. These trends come by due to the interaction of the buyer and the seller. The aggressiveness of one of the parties in the market will determine how steep the trend becomes. To make a profit, you have to take advantage of the changes in the price movement.

To understand the direction of the trend, you ought to look at the troughs and peaks and how they relate to each other.

When looking for money in options trading, you ought to trade with a trend. The trend is what determines the decision you make when faced with a situation – whether to buy or to sell. You need to know the various signs that a prevailing trend is soon ending so that you can manage the risks and exit the trades the right way.

Characteristics of Technical Analysis

This analysis makes use of models and trading rules using different price and volume changes. These include the volume, price, and other different market info.

Technical analysis is applied among financial professionals and traders and is used by many option traders.

The Principles of Technical analysis

Many traders on the market use the price to come up with information that affects the decision you make ultimately. The analysis looks at the trading pattern and what information it offers you rather than looking at drivers such as news events, economic and fundamental events.

Price action usually tends to change every time because the investor leans towards a certain pattern, which in turn predicts trends and conditions.

Prices Determine Trends

Technical analysts know that the price in the market determines the trend of the market. The trend can be up, down, or move sideways.

History Usually Repeats Itself

Analysts believe that an investor repeats the behavior of the people that traded before them. The investor sentiment usually repeats itself. Due to the fact that the behavior repeats itself, traders know that using a price pattern can lead to predictions.

The investor uses the research to determine if the trend will continue or if the reversal will stop eventually and will anticipate a change when the charts show a lot of investor sentiment.

Combination with Other Analysis Methods

To make the most out of the technical analysis, you need to combine it with other charting methods on the market. You also need to use secondary data, such as sentiment analysis and indicators.

To achieve this, you need to go beyond pure technical analysis, and combine other market forecast methods in line with technical work. You can use technical analysis along with fundamental analysis to improve the performance of your portfolio.

You can also combine technical analysis with economics and quantitative analysis. For instance, you can use neural networks along with technical analysis to identify the relationships in the market. Other traders make use of technical analysis with astrology.

Other traders go for newspaper polls, sentiment indicators to come with deductions.

The Different Types of Charts Used in Technical Analysis

Candlestick Chart

This is a charting method that came from the Japanese. The method fills the interval between opening and closing prices to show a relationship. These candles use color coding to show the closing points. You will come across black, red, white, blue, or green candles to represent the closing point at any time.

Open-high-low-close Chart (OHLC)

These are also referred to as bar charts, and they give you a connection between the maximum and minimum prices in a trading period. They usually feature a tick on the left side to show the open price and one on the right to show the closing price.

Line Chart

This is a chart that maps the closing price values using a line segment.

Point and Figure Chart

This employs numerical filters that reference times without fully using the time to construct the chart.

Overlays

These are usually used on the main price charts and come in different ways:

- *Resistance* – refers to a price level that acts as the maximum level above the usual price

- *Support* – the opposite of resistance, and it shows as the lowest value of the price

- *Trend line* – this is a line that connects two troughs or peaks.

- *Channel* – refers to two trend lines that are parallel to each other

- *Moving average* – a kind of dynamic trend line that looks at the average price in the market

- *Bollinger bands* – these are charts that show the rate of volatility in a market.

- *Pivot point* – this refers to the average of the high, low, and closing price averages for a certain stock or currency.

Price-based Indicators

These analyze the price values of the market. These include:

• *Advance decline line* – this is an indicator of the market breadth

• *Average directional index* – shows the strength of a trend in the market

• *Commodity channel index* – helps you to identify cyclical trends in the market

• *Relative strength index* – this is a chart that shows you the strength of the price

• *Moving average convergence (MACD)* – this shows the point where two trend line converge or diverge.

• *Stochastic oscillator* – this shows the close position that has happened within the recent trading range

• *Momentum* – this is a chart that tells you how fast the price changes

The Benefits of Technical Analysis in Options Trading

There are a variety of benefits that you enjoy when you use technical analysis in trading options. The benefits arise from the fact that traders are usually asking a lot of questions touching on the price of the market and entry points. While the forecast for prices is a huge task, the use of technical analysis makes it easier to handle.

The major advantages of technical analysis include

Expert Trend Analysis

This is the biggest advantage of technical analysis in any market. With this method, you can predict the direction of the market at any time. You can determine whether the market will move up, down or sideways easily.

Entry and Exit Points

As a trader, you need to know when to place a trade and when to opt out. The entry point is all about knowing the right time to enter the trade for good returns. Exiting a trade is also vital because it allows you to reduce losses.

Leverage Early Signals

Every trader looks for ways to get early signals to assist them in making decisions. Technical analysis gives you signals to trigger a decision on your part. This is usually ideal when you suspect that a trend will reverse soon. Remember the time the trend reverses are when you need to make crucial decisions.

It Is Quick

In options trading, you need to go with techniques that give you fast results. Additionally, getting technical analysis data is cheaper than other techniques in fundamental analysis, with some companies offering free charting programs. If you are in the market to make use of short time intervals such as 1-minute, 5-minute, 30 minute or 1-hour charts, you can get this using technical analysis.

It Gives You A Lot of Information

Technical analysis gives you a lot of information that you can use to make trading decisions. You can easily build a position depending on the information you get then take or exit trades. You have access to information such as chart pattern, trends, support, resistance, market momentum, and other information.

The current price of an asset usually reflects every known information of an asset. While the market might be rife with rumors that the prices might surge or plummet, the current price represents the final point for all information. As the traders and investors change their bearing from one part to another, the changes in asset reflect the current value perception.

If all this turns out to be true, then the only info you require is a price chart that gives all the price reflections and predictions. There isn't any need for you to worry yourself with the reasons why the price is rising or falling when you can use a chart to determine everything.

With the right technical analysis information, you can make trading easier and faster because you make decisions based not on hearsay but facts. You don't have to spend your time reading and trying to make headway in financial news. All you need us to check what the chart tells you.

You Understand Trends

If the prices on the market were to gyrate randomly without any direction, you would find it hard to make money. While these trends run in all directions, the prices always move in trends. Directional bias allows you to leverage the benefits of making money. Technical analysis allows you to determine when a trend occurs and when it doesn't occur, or when it is in reversal.

Many of the profitable techniques that are used by the traders to make money follow trends. This means that you find the right trend and then look for opportunities that allow you to enter the market in the same direction as the trend. This helps you to capitalize on the price movement.

Trends run in various degrees. The degree of the trend determines how much money you make, whether in the short term or long-term trading. Technical analysis gives you all the tools that make it possible for you to do this.

History Always Repeats Itself

Technical analysis uses common patterns to give you the information to trade. However, you need to understand that history will not be exact when it repeats itself, though. The current analysis will be either bigger or smaller, depending on the existing market conditions. The only thing is that it won't be a replica of the prior pattern.

This pans out easily because most human psychology doesn't change so much, and you will see that the emotions have a hand in making sure that prices rise and fall. The emotions that traders exhibit create a lot of patterns that lead to changes in prices all the time. As a trader, you need to identify these patterns and then use them for trading. Use prior history to guide you and then the current price as a trigger of the trade.

Enjoy Proper Timing

Do you know that without proper timing you will not be able to make money at all? One of the major advantages of technical analysis is that you get the chance to time the trades. Using technical analysis, you get to wait, then place your money in other opportunities until it is the right time to place a trade.

Applicable Over a Wide Time Frame

When you learn technical analysis, you get to apply it to many areas in different markets, including options. All the trading in a market is based mostly on the patters that are as a result of human behavior. These patterns can then be mapped out on a chart to be used across the markets.

While there is some difference between analyzing different securities, you will be able to use technical analysis in most of the markets.

Additionally, you can use the analysis in any timeframe, which is applicable whether you use hourly, daily, or weekly charts. These markets are usually taken to be fractal, which essentially means that patterns that appear on a small scale will also be present on a large scale as well.

Technical Analysis Secrets to Become the Best Trader

To make use of technical analysis the right way, you need to follow time-testing approaches that have made the technique a gold mine for many traders. Let us look at the various tips that will take you from novice to pro in just a few days:

Use More than One Indicator

Numbers make trading easy, but it also applies to the way you apply your techniques. For one, you need to know that just because one technical indicator is better than using one, applying a second indicator is better than using just one. The use of more than one indicator is one of the best ways to confirm a trend. It also increases the odds of being right.

As a trader, you will never be 100 percent right at all times, and you might even find that the odds are stashed against you when everything is plain to see. However, don't demand too much from your indicators such that you end up with analysis paralysis.

To achieve this, make use of indicators that complement each other rather than the ones that clash against each other.

Go For Multiple Time Frames

Using the same buy signal every day allows you to have confidence that the indicator is giving you all you need to know to trade. However, make sure you look for a way to use multiple timeframes to confirm a trend. When you have a doubt, it is wise that you increase the timeframe from an hour to a day or from a daily chart to a weekly chart.

Understand that No Indicator Measures Everything

You need to know that indicators are supposed to show how strong a trend is, they won't tell you much more. So, you need to understand and focus on what the indicator is supposed to communicate instead of working with assumptions.

Go With the Trend

If you notice that an option is trading upward, then go ahead and buy it. Conversely when the trend stops trending, then it is time to sell it. If you aren't sure of what is going on in the market at that time, then don't make a move.

However, waiting might make you lose profitable trades as opposed to trading. You also miss out on opportunities to create more capital.

Have the Right Skills

It really takes superior analytical capabilities and real skill to be successful at trading, just like any other endeavor. Many people think that it is hard to make money with options trading, but with the right approach, you can make extraordinary profits.

You need to learn and understand the various skills so that you know what the market seeks from you and how to achieve your goals.

Trade with a Purpose

Many traders go into options trading with the main aim of having a hobby. Well, this way you won't be able to make any money at all. What you need to do is to trade for the money – strive to make profits unlike those who try to make money as a hobby.

Always Opt for High value

Well, no one tells you to trade any security that comes your way – it is purely a matter of choice. Try and go for high-value options so that you can trade them the right way. Make use of fundamental analysis to choose the best options to trade in.

Be Disciplined

When using technical analysis, you might find yourself in situations that require you to make a decision fast. To achieve success, you need to have strict risk management protocols. Don't base on your track record to come up with choices; instead, make sure you follow what the analysis tells you.

Don't Overlook Your Trading Plan

The trading plan is in place to guide you when things go awry. Coming up with the plan is easy, but many people find it hard to implement the plan the right way. The trading plan has various components – the signals and the take-profit/stop-loss rules. Once you get into the market, you need to control yourself because you have already taken a leap. Remember you cannot control the indicators once they start running – all you can do is to prevent yourself from messing up everything.

Come up with the trading rules when you are unemotional to try and mitigate the effects of making bad decisions.

Accept Losses

Many people trade with one thing in mind – losses aren't part of their plan. This is a huge mistake because you need to understand that every trade has two sides to it – a loss and a profit. Remember that the biggest mistake that leads to losses isn't anything to do with bad indicators rather using them the wrong way. Always have a stop-loss order when you trade to prevent loss of money.

Have a Target When You Trade

So, what do you plan to achieve today? Remember, trading is a way to grow your capital as opposed to saving. Options trading is a business that has probable outcomes that you get to estimate. When you make a profit, make sure you take some money from the table and then put it in a safe place.

How to Apply Technical Analysis

Many traders have heard of technical analysis, but they don't know how to use it to make deductions and come up with decisions that impact their trades. Here are the different steps to make sure you have the right decision when you use technical analysis.

1. Identify a Trend

You need to identify an option and then see whether there is a trend or not. The trend might be driving the options up or down. The market is bullish if it is moving up and bearish when it is moving down. As a trader, you need to go along with the trend instead of fighting it. When you fight against the trend, you incur unnecessary losses that will make it hard to achieve the rewards that you seek.

You also need to have good ways to identify the trend; this is because the market has the capacity to move in a certain direction. It is not all about identifying the direction of the trend but also when the trend is moving out of the trend.

So, how can you identify a trend the right way? Here are some tools to use so as to get the right trend:

Vertical Call Spreads

Call spreads require less upfront capital than the previous strategies we've looked at, the collar and the covered call. While the covered call is a steady income earner for the main long position and the collar works with speculative and investment positions, call spreads are purely speculative.

The vertical in the name refers to the way the trade is structured and how it presents itself when viewed as part of the option chain. Options spread trades are a slightly more advanced form of trading and prior to getting into these strategies, it is best if you gain a thorough understanding of the collar and make steady income with it.

Bull Call Spread

The bull call spread enables you to make money in up trending markets. The beauty of this strategy is that you can adjust your spread on the basis of the level of market bullishness, with more bullish markets requiring a high speed and mildly bullish ones requiring a lower spread.

The trade consists of two legs, a long call and a short call with the same expiration month. The long call should be close to or at the money and is the primary instrument for profit in this strategy. The short call should be decided on the same principles as the short on the covered call, with a strike price just far enough to provide a good premium but not too close that the market price would breach it.

As you can imagine the strike price levels depend heavily on the level of bullishness of the market. Generally speaking, it is a good idea to place your short call just beyond a strong resistance level. Let's look at how the numbers work with an example.

Profit and Loss Numbers

Walmart, WMT, is currently trading at $110.62. Let's assume a bullish outlook for the stock but not a heavily bullish one. Assuming we set an exit time of a month for this trade to work out within, the August 110 call, which is technically at the money will cost us $2.44 to purchase. Alternatively, you could also purchase the 112 call which can be had for $1.41. Let's go with the latter since this reduces our cost basis.

For the short call, given that our outlook is only for a month, a strike price of 120 seems reasonable since to hit this level a gain of 9% is necessary which seems unlikely to happen in just a month. The premium we receive for this option is $0.04. Thus, our numbers are:

Cost of trade entry = Premium paid for 112 call - premium received for 120 call = 1.41-.04 = $1.37.

This also happens to be our maximum risk on this trade. If the market price of the stock decreases, the long call will expire worthless but the short call premium will remain the same and thus cap our risk.

Maximum reward = Strike price of short call - Strike price of long call - Premium paid for long call + Premium received for short call = 120-112-1.41+0.04 = $6.63

This gives us a very tidy 4.43 reward to risk ratio which any directional trader would give an arm and a leg for. You can increase the profit potential by laying around with the long call strike price but remember that your short call strike has to be taken into account as well.

Furthermore, you will also need to place your strike prices at sensible levels with respect to S/R zones. Your short call should ideally be beyond a strong resistance level or if your outlook is a month or less, beyond some level which is sure to give pause to price and delay its advance past it. The best level for a short call would be right at the resistance level since any price beyond this will result in an opportunity loss and any level below this will result in a less than maximum reward.

What if the market turns out to behave in the exact opposite manner than what you predicted? Well, in that case, you will need to adjust your trade by either moving your spread to lower levels, that is, picking lower strike prices for both legs and switching to a bear call spread strategy which we'll look at in the next section.

All in all, the bull call spread relies on you reading market conditions correctly and more importantly, picking the right strike prices in line with S/R zones. If you happen to see price in a range, then using the bottom boundary as the long strike price and the top boundary as the short strike price is an excellent method to make money every month.

Start by implementing this in ranges and then progress to slow moving trends. Only once you've mastered these should you move onto fast trends.

Bear Call Spread

The bear call spread is designed to take advantage of bearish market situations. Now, keep in mind that in addition to bearish overall conditions, you can also make use of this strategy in ranging conditions, such as at the top of the range.

If you find a price at or near the top boundary of a range then implementing this strategy with a shorter term expectation for it to work will bring you good profits in the short run. The key as always is to ensure that your risk is covered and that your strike prices are in line with S/R environment.

The bear call, just like the bull call, has two legs to it. There is a short call and a long call but in the bear call spread's case, the short call is below the long call. The higher strike price long call caps our maximum risk while the short leg functions as the primary profit generator.

The short call should be at the money or as close to it as possible with the long call just beyond a strong S/R level. Let's look via an example how the numbers work for this strategy.

Profit and Loss Numbers

Sticking with good old' WMT, we have a market price of $110.62 as of previous close. Let's assume this is at the top of a range currently and we expect the range to hold.

Mind you, we don't know for sure which is why every trade needs risk mitigation.

You first step is to buy a call with a strike price beyond the resistance level. This will give you premium income and obviously, the closer it is to the market price, the more income you will earn. Of course, the danger of having it too close is that a momentary spike might jeopardize your strategy so you need to balance it out.

Let's say that 115 is a good level and that we expect this to hold for at least a month. The August 115 call costs us $0.50 to buy.

Next, we sell a call which is as close to the money as possible. As with the bull call spread, let's pick the 112 level which will provide us with $1.32 in premium income. As a side note: the prices I've quoted for the 112 strike price option is different because remember that when you buy, you pay the ask price and when you sell, you pay the bid. In this case $1.32 is the bid price.

Our number work out as:

Maximum gain/cost of trade entry= Premium from short call - Premium from long call = 1.32-0.4= $0.92

Maximum loss= Strike price of long call - Strike price of short call - cost of trade entry = 115-112-0.92=$2.08

As you can see, this trade has a reward risk ratio of just 0.44. However, this is still a profitable strategy due to the fact that the win rate is usually quite high with this strategy. Recall the win rate and average win calculations we performed in the chapter on risk and you can figure out what win rate is required to break even and profit on this strategy.

Even this strategy can be adjusted to higher spread levels should you choose but this should be done only if the S/R and the market environment supports readjustment. If you misread a bear trend and the market starts becoming bullish, adjustment is not going to do anything for you.

Both the spread trades require you to read market conditions thoroughly and this why I recommend starting out with covered calls and collars which are market neutral. Despite the lower risk levels of the vertical spread trades, you will have to incur a higher level of directionality with them and this exposes you to further risk.

The bear call spread is a good example of this. Given the high win rate it needs to make you money, it is far less forgiving of mistakes than other strategies. Thus, you need to have a very high level of market and order flow deciphering skills, coupled with the right mindset.

There is money to be made but you need to build the correct foundation before progressing forward.

Advanced Strategies and Techniques

Some things to know about Calls and Puts:

Calls are used for bullish markets. They are utilized when you assume the option is going up.

Puts are used during a bearish market. They work best when you believe the stock is going lower and you need to protect yourself from a great loss.

It can mean the difference between a $50,000 loss and a $5,000 loss. You're getting out before the story gets even rougher. You can even make money with a Put. Your strike can ensure that you sell a stock at a certain price, which ends up being a higher amount than what the stock is actually worth. The one main rule to this strategy is that the investor never forgets that everything in Options Trading has an expiration date. If you fail to handle your Call or Put within the specified time, everything expires.

Image of a Call Option in action
(Courtesy, www.investorglossary.com)

Grow A Small Account into Something Bigger:

There are a couple of ways of building your portfolio by using Options Trading. The first one is by purchasing a large number of contracts, maybe 10 to 20, at a low price. This is very important, that the stocks must be low-priced stocks, because Putting an Option on one large stock isn't likely to yield much for you. Variety here is very important. Think of it like this: When a contractor goes to work on a home does he take only a hammer with him? No. He takes an entire toolbox. He might even take several truckloads of tools and other workers to assist him. Why? Because the success of his business depends on the variety of tools he has at the ready. If he only has one great hammer, he can only do one thing at a time. It's the same with Options Trading. If you're going to make a living doing this, or if you're going to grow your portfolio to a size that benefits you financially, you're going to need to Put Options on a large number of low price stocks, in the same way the housing contractor invests in a lot of small tools to make a much bigger business success for himself than one expertly designed hammer can do.

So, what's a low priced stock? Maybe a stock that moves up about $1.00 within a thirty day period. Purchase smaller contracts for those stocks that seem to be moving quickly, but steadily. You don't want to purchase something that has fallen sharply, picked up quickly, and fallen sharply again. Another great analogy for assessing whether or not a stock is a decent one is to think of dieting. Research shows us that those people who diet extremely, who lose more than 10lbs in a week's time, gain it back twice as fast when the diet is over. Stocks can be measured in a similar way. The sudden loss and gain is always something to measure with caution. Did the stock fall sharply in the last 30 days? Is it climbing back up in a measured pattern? Maybe by $1.00 to $3.00 every thirty day period? Then this is probably a stock that's worth taking a look at, and maybe, even Putting an Option on.

Remember, an Option is just a contract. We use Options in all sorts of areas in our everyday lives. We pay a monthly premium on health insurance. Maybe we spend $150-$300 a month on a health insurance plan that covers our check-ups, emergency room visits, and surgeries. Most of the time, nothing serious happens, but does this mean that most people are fine without having health insurance? No way. Why? Because everything could be fine for 25 years of your life. You could, literally, only ever had a cold, but when you fall down the stairs one day and break your arm, you suddenly find yourself needing to make an emergency room visit. Just to get in the door, it's several hundred dollars. The initial nurse triage is another hundred dollars. Then, after hours of waiting, you get into one of the emergency room beds and a new nurse sees you and hooks you up to an IV. Gives you some pain meds. Another doctor comes in to see you. Orders more tests. Now your bill has skyrocketed into the thousands. The person who has health insurance may complain that they have to pay a monthly premium of $300 just to cover one 25-year-old who's never sick, but that complaining ends the day they break their arm and, $10,000 later, they walk out of the emergency room only having to pay the $100 copay.

Sample of exercising the Put Option
(Courtesy, www.learn-stock-options-trading.com)

This is why insurance is so important. It's the same with Options Trading. Why would you throw $10,000 at a stock, watch it crash, and maybe walk away another $20,000 in the hole a month later? This is why Options are important. Yes, they come with risk, but only as much risk as you contract yourself to lose. If you've placed a $100 Put on a Strike, then when that stock falls, you're out only $100 per share, and not, say $500 like someone else.

Another good example of why Options are important when protecting your portfolio is to think of real estate. Say you're looking for a new home and you've been pre-approved for a $300,000 loan. The guy across the street is going to sell his home for exactly $300,000. Awesome. But you're not sure that you want to buy the house for that amount yet. You don't want to be roped into several hundred thousand dollars of debt until you see how other things are selling around the neighborhood. Maybe, you can end up buying the house for less in the end. So, you offer your neighbor a contract, an Option. You say, "I'll pay $3,000 today, non-refundable, if you promise not to sell this house to anyone else within the next 30 days, and you sell this house to me for $300,000 no matter what else is happening to the housing market in this neighborhood at the end of that time period." You tell your neighbor that this contract binds you to buy this house within 30 days or to walk away having lost $3,000. Your neighbor considers the offer, thinks it makes pretty good sense, and you sign on the dotted line.

This could go one of two ways: In the next thirty days, the house next door to your neighbor's could be sold, without a realtor, to a family member just for the price of the mortgage, and there's only $20,000 left on the mortgage. No profit is made because of this low sale, and it brings down the value of every home on the street. This includes your neighbor's house, which is now only worth $250,000, but if you really love it, and you buy it, you're going to pay $50,000 above market and you'll be throwing much of your money away. So, what do you do? You safely walk away. Yes, you're losing that $3,000 that you saved up all last summer, but you're not stuck in a $300,000 upside down mortgage. Now which one would give you greater heartburn? The upside down mortgage in a neighborhood that's going down in value, or the loss of $3,000 which, if you saved it last summer, you could save it again this summer?

The other thing that could happen in this Options scenario is that the guy's house you're interested in buying could have a windfall. The house next to it could sell to, not a family member but a stranger, and this person could be absolutely in love with the place. She could offer the seller $450,000 just for the gift of living in your neighborhood, and now you can purchase your dream home within that 30 day timeframe for only $300,000. That house has gone up in value now, too, maybe even by $100,000. You can buy that house for a steal, sell it at a much higher price, and make a profit. Options protect your financial future in much the same way that insurance does. So, now that you see how Options are used in everyday life, you can get a better insider understanding of how they work in the financial world as well.

Make Binary Options Trading Simple Through a Broker

With the idea of globalization, the development of the business substances has come to even the country and remove fragments of the globe. In this day and age, it has turned out to be especially apparent for a nation to go into international exchanging for worldwide acknowledgment. The equivalent is the situation with the paired choices exchanging which trading is performed on the stocks and items in the financial markets. The benefit just as misfortune circumstance in the twofold exchanging is subject to the development in the cost of the shares or products. As the world's economy is creating a wide margin, the parallel transferring can be a worthwhile exchanging if execute with a careful examination by the speculator.

The capacity of Binary Trading Brokers
Paired exchanging has turned into the most common exchanging platform, and because of the quick thriving of this business, development in parallel alternatives intermediaries' quality is occurring. The significance of the representatives can't be disregarded as the real job of the agent is to deliberately deal with the exchange of

the speculator by managing him through each thick and slender of twofold exchange. Behind the achievement of each transaction, the binary choices intermediary is the first column. With the appearance of new representative elements in the international business platform, it has turned out to be much simpler to choose the best specialist as indicated by the inclination. The agent enables the financial specialist in taking the best choice at the ideal planning to keep away from the misfortune and limit the dangers.

Cash and Risk Management by The Binary Options Broker

Merchant in parallel alternatives exchanging has the total specialist to choose the benefit and plan the cash the executive's strategy. It is the parallel alternatives dealer who directs the broker in the best conceivable manner concerning the advantage type that is best for exchanging. The help of the agent has a great deal of significant worth as he is knowledgeable about the field of exchanging and is proficient in his methodology. For the long haul advantages and benefits to the financial specialist, it would be the best plan to take help from the representative. Double alternatives agent diminishes the merchant in great occasions by furnishing with the best counter-strategies to make tremendous result from each exchange. Dealers, who are particularly keen on building up a fruitful career in parallel exchanging world, never stay away from the administrations and help of the best twofold agent.

Winning In The Currency Options Trading Market

When trading monetary standards on the Forex showcase, an incredible method to shield yourself from unexpected, unpredictable changes in the market is to purchase currency alternatives. When you are buying a choice from an intermediary, you agree with that handle that gives the privilege or "choice" to buy sell or do nothing at a foreordained cost. Currency choices can have extraordinary potential for noteworthy increases with restricted hazard. In the accompanying part, we will investigate a couple of the procedures that make options trading so appealing.

Before we plunge into currency choices trading systems, you should realize that trading in a universal market, for example, the forex, includes trillions of dollars consistently. The universe of the global fund can and is a confused organization with incredible opportunities to make and lose a lot of cash quick. I implore you to master everything that you can about the market you choose to enter and make a few papers or practice exchanges "sham" account before taking a chance with your assets. You can discover numerous books, instructive courses, and essential data online or however your intermediary or venture instructor.

System #1

Keep time on your side.

Purchase choices in large slanting markets with additional time. The extra time you have in the decision the better possibility you need to make counter "puts" or "calls" supporting your position. You will pay a premium for these choices at the same time, the time you put resources into can receive extraordinary benefits.

Methodology #2

Purchase at or close to the cash with almost 90 percent of all alternatives terminating out of the money each day, be one of the 10% and purchase choices that are "in cash" or at the cash. Keep in mind a long shot can make pleasant increases, however until that cash is in your record, that is all that it is, potential. Purchasing in or at the money will enable you to set aside a few minutes.

I trust these procedures give you a superior thought of how to approach currency alternatives. These techniques are over improved and only two of numerous ways you can use to expand your chances of getting more cash in the outside currency showcase. At whatever point conceivable you ought to receive the mentality; it is smarter to take numerous little increases over a significant lot of time than hazard it all on a long shot.

Currency Forex Online Trading For Newbies

This is kind of an amateur's manual for the Forex showcase, for any individual who is keen on dunking their hands in a trillion dollar daily venture commercial center that can profit for anybody willing enough to buckle down out it an attempt. While the Forex advertises is viewed as a standout amongst the best contributing choices for merchants of products, there are as yet inborn entanglements and things that everybody ought to keep away from before they begin developing their venture portfolio. Getting off on the right foot will imply that the remainder of your adventure will be smooth and inconvenience free. This is the manual for currency Forex online trading for novices.

Right off the bat, you need to comprehend the market, which implies understanding the ware you will manage; currency. The Forex showcase manages a single action - the purchasing and selling of money for the express reason for profiting. This is done when you do spot purchasing of currency (or any purchasing). Your cash goes into the nation or the nation's stakes; which implies your money can go the world over in only seconds and it very well may be utilized for any one thing which incorporates; reinforcing of speculative stock investments, infrastructural support, supporting financial activities or even primarily as a formative activity. The conceivable outcomes are unfathomable; however, what happens is that you will reinforce the nation's financial position and accordingly raise the estimation of their dollar. When that occurs, you make a moment benefit from the PIP (rate in point) increment. The more positive PIPs you click, the more cash you are likely going to make. More or less, a straightforward nutshell; this is the essential apparatus of the Forex trading market.

The Forex showcase works 24 hours every day and this implies contributing has no rest assigned to it. Be set up to be woken up by your agent at some odd hour to let you know of a venture chance of the century. Online trading likewise implies that you can get to the market from anyplace and wherever on the planet; all using a PC. I think the most comfortable route for a novice to begin is to agree to accept anybody of the realized financier firms online. They give thorough preparing to anybody needing to gain proficiency with the essentials of Forex trading and have even sham records with phony cash and reenacted circumstances for you to tinker around with before you plunge into the genuine article. Likewise, a significant number of these organizations will also either give or offer you a Forex Trading Systems programming, which is essentially a stage that makes trading even more straightforward. With a professional layout, callouts and data showed ergonomically; these frameworks are indispensable for the beginner to discover his or her way around the commercial center. Further developed structures exhort novices on their speculation moves and right their wrongs on the spot.

Trading Options - Learn How to Trade Options

Today the quantity of examiners who attempt their karma in choice exchanging is unmistakably uncovering an ascent. Dissimilar to stocks that may result in a noteworthy hit to your financial position, the most extreme misfortune while transferring opportunities are restricted to the sum you paid for the chance. To begin with, online choices exchanging contact an intermediary who charges a sensible commission for his administrations and offer clues on the ideal approach to perform decisions exchanging. A portion of the representatives provides you with a stage to figure out how to trade alternatives utilizing sham instruments until you figure out how to ace it. This is without a doubt an incredible method to increase most extreme financial influence while managing the genuine devices.

Making a benefit in the present volatile market is intense and testing. With the swing to be taken by the market staying unusual to a more significant degree to many, it is continuously smarter to move to exchange investment opportunities. Exchanging alternatives carefully pursue some essential methodologies that make supernatural occurrences even in the fluctuating business sector situation. The players of choice exchanging can incorporate the different techniques implied for the bearish just as the bullish markets to appreciate most extreme influence. A portion of the significant decisions exchanging methodologies included bull call spread, and the bull put spread techniques in the bullish markets;

short straddle, short choke, proportion spreads, long condor and long butterfly in a precarious bearish market situation; and guts, butterfly, condor, straddle, choke, or hazard inversion where one wants to play a nonpartisan turn in exchanging choice when he is unconscious of the contort to be taken by the market.

It isn't only the methodologies that characterize the accomplishment of alternative dealers, for both the essayist and examiner of choice exchanging. Different components that control the progression of exchanging alternatives are:

1. One when to purchase or sell the options as past its expiry, the other options are nothing, yet a squandering resource with zero esteem.
2. Volatile supplies of reliable organizations that are certain to yield more significant premium instead of different organizations.

Highly fluid alternatives that are exchanged with most extreme energy in the market moving over various hands to appreciate most enormous influence, not at all like illiquid resources that are to stamp a hit to the financial situation.

Continuously play with the cash you can manage the cost of as too hazardous an endeavor will make a gap to your current financial standing. Each stock picked by you for the alternative needs to appreciate more prominent value movements offer most extreme unpredictability, or more all, must be reasonable to make it an active exchange.

The Non-Directional Trading Formula and Other Types of Trading

A few people may discover financial market exchanging, for example, outside trade exchanging, and fates advertise exchanging, forex choices exchanging, securities exchange exchanging, and so forth., as something terrifying. This is for the straightforward reason that the terminologies and the procedures may sound excessively mind-boggling. Notwithstanding, exchanging comes down to just three sorts. The dimensions of trouble likewise vary.

The most popular sort, additionally the least demanding of the three is the sort that goes with the pattern. This is likewise considered the directional exchanging technique that is additionally viewed as the customary methodology. It trusts that movement in the financial market takes just a single direction thereby making it unsurprising. Brokers oblige the pattern as dependent on the past information assembled. A few methodologies that fall under this sort are the "Sacred Grail" set up, the spurious exchanging, retracement type and a break-out variety.

The following kind is the one that counters the pattern. It conflicts with the group and anticipates an adjustment in direction. Many would not consent to a sort that battles the model yet this has demonstrated to have worked for some merchants especially those that pick tops and bottoms, as it were. This is a real method for gaining benefits in the exchanging industry and many sticks to this technique.

The last and most convoluted sort is the utilization of the non directional exchanging equations and methodologies. This is the most developed; however numerous speculators discover it very unpredictable. It is likewise tough to execute and needs much computerization. It is hard to understand yet learning it will be to the financial specialist's advantage since it is the perfect sort for a market that moves in numerous direction and is very erratic. The present economic situation of the world makes this chaotic movement in the market conceivable. Let that not hose your spirits and keep making benefits with the utilization of a non directional exchanging recipe.

Aspects of Currency Online Trading That Can Benefit You

This is the most fluid market on the planet. This is the reason you ought to consider going into currency online trading. The more significant part of the more traditional markets on the earth today have an element which can be very inconvenient to trading, and this is the way that it has a lot of formality and procedures that will back you off somewhat. These red tapes can now and then bind you and see the market move past you. When you have a fluid market, you can then settle on the choice and after that examine the market responds to your preference. Making cash is always about speed and speed is something that isn't an element of a portion of the markets out there. This is the reason you ought to consider the Forex market, the liquidity and the over the counter nature will make it an excellent choice for you.

Next, the online currency trading is additionally a lose-lose situation which implies that there will dependably be a champ and dependably be a failure. What isolates the two gatherings of speculators is that one gathering buckles down and has a decent methodology set up. This implies you will dependably get the opportunity to profit on the Forex market. Buckle down, have an adequate framework set up and pick the correct merchant. You likewise need to settle on which sort of venture strategy you are OK with. When you have this in your grasp, at that point, you will have a decent day at the market, and you will before long end up the correct way. In the most noticeably awful and the best of times, there will dependably be champs in the Forex market. You should put yourself in the correct market bearing, and soon you will profit.

The exact opposite thing you ought to consider about the Forex market is that there are incredible frameworks of help out there, regardless of whether you are a novice financial specialist who has no clue about the market. These can be considered under the class of dummy accounts, guidebooks, and intermediary preparing accounts. These things will assist you with gaining close information about the market and therefore, commit the errors you need and learn from them without losing genuine cash. When you take a few to get back some composure on the market, something you can do is to see it or not the market is directly for you. Likewise, you will also have the option to find out about the market and base your system (starting) on these dummy accounts.

These are a portion of the things that you should think about currency trading. One of the words about this market is that it considers the easygoing and the retail financial specialist to turn out and profit that full-time brokers are in the market. Along these lines, while thinking about which stage to get into and put your cash at, at that point the Forex market ought to be one of the alternatives you consider.

Find out About the Basics OF Forex Trading

Forex or Foreign Exchange Trading alludes to the trading of monetary standards of various nations against one another. The trading is regularly done through specialists in a relentless money market. The dealers make or free cash out of synchronous purchasing and selling of monetary forms in worldwide just as neighborhood markets. The instrument utilized for the exchange is a proportion between the estimations of the two financial types to be exchanged, ordinarily known as the conversion standard or the forex rate.

Forex trading is directed in a market which gloats of exceptionally high liquidity. There is no time limit - the market is open 24 hours every day amid all the working days. This is a worldwide market which encourages trading with every free currency of the world. The idea of the market is precariously making it conceivable to profit, exploiting the quickly evolving prospects. The progressions are generally achieved by specific components like dangerous obligations and so forth.

Like in some other business, dangers are natural in such trading too. This is because trading here depends on the theory which in no uncertainty increases the hazard. There is a wellbeing statement here which you can work out, for example by setting a breaking point which as it were is to characterize the most extreme misfortune when the markets conflict with you.

Zero commission trading gives different choices, and there is a plausibility for substantial volume trading regardless of whether your capital base is generally low. Today such trading is significantly progressively rearranged with the appearance of the web and the online forex trading alternatives. You can get a ton of information online and furthermore set up a dummy record and work on trading with it before you choose to go live.

Forex-trading is embraced by corporate gatherings who exchange millions and furthermore by little scale brokers who begin off with a few hundred and enjoy forex smaller than expected trading. A great deal can be picked up from the world's largest currency trading market with a touch of tolerance and understanding.

Options Trading Risk Strategies

Partaking in options trading, there are some risk management options that can help you invest better and will make things better for you. This chapter will go over nine specific things to watch out for when options trading, and why each of these nine options are important in options trading. You should be able to use this in order to obtain consistency in options trading, along with considerable success.

Allocation Flows Downstream

The first concept is to go over asset allocation. You should make sure that you aren't putting everything intone thing. You should make sure that you're not putting your entire investment portfolio into equities, but also into bonds, real estate, and commodities. You should also work to make sure that the diversification applies to classes as well.

Many start thinking that they are going to only put their options into equities such as Apple or Google. However, if you're not putting it in other places, it will make your portfolio become too weighted in one area. You should also make sure that it's not overlapping with one another as well, such as if you own both stocks and mutual funds.

You should look at the company and what they hold before investing in it, because you might end up investing too much into one area.

The reason why you should watch for this and make sure that you allocate effectively is because the more diverse a portfolio means that there will be less swings or losses when volatility happens. In recent years however, the downturns can be correlated, so make sure that if you're investing, don't put everything into one market. If you put everything in real estate, it can end up ruining you, such as the case of many investors during the 2008 housing bubble burst.

The Importance of Differences

Options that are diversified actually can make a difference in a portfolio. Options, especially ones that are volatile, can be seen as a class. They can also be used to protect you overall. You can use ETFs to help with this, and it can be helpful when it comes to hedging. Having a different portfolio can help you prevent anything awry from happening, and it can also show that you're in a good position in case if things go bad.

Watching Overall Risk Capital

You need to watch out for the overall risk capital. If you're trading options, you should watch for it increasing above 15-20% of the overall risk capital. This is because if you let it exceed, you're putting yourself at risk and you might have too much on the table. You will also need to plan in case if the stop-loss happens to you, you might lose more of your capital than expected. That's why you should make sure that your portfolio only has that much, and if it exceeds act accordingly.

Watch Option Account

If you have an option account, you need to watch how much is on the market. You should make sure that no more than 50% is on the market at any time. It's risky to even have 50% on the market, so it might be best to have less than that when you can.

Watch Singularities

For a single option, you should make sure that it doesn't represent more than 5% of the options portfolio on the risk side. If that position starts to fail, it will not hurt you if it's that number. That's because it can usually go down to about 2.5%, which is only a 50% loss. It's better to make sure you don't put too much into one area than to rely on one option to save it all.

Trade How You're Comfortable

The problem with many beginner traders, is that they don't trade with what they're comfortable with. Many credit products are hard to understand, but the bigger issue at hand is that they are double-leveraged products. Many who are beginning are not comfortable with their construction and behavior. You should make sure that you know how you're working with the product, because if you're not familiar enough with it, you're not going to get anywhere with it. It can save you if you keep this risk management strategy in, and as you combine this with learning, it can make your ability to trade options that much better.

Manage your Money

Managing money is vital for this. You only have a certain amount to use, so you have to keep control of it in order to prevent it from being lost forever. The best thing to do is to position-size, which is when you decide how much you want to enter into any options trade. By doing this, you can determine how much you want to invest, and how much of a percentage you will put into something. You should only use a small amount so you're not relying on one outcome. Some trades can turn out bad, but if you manage it right and only put a certain amount into it, you'll be able to decide how much you're going to put in and how bad the possible risks can be.

Top Mistakes made by New Traders

Swing trading isn't as risky as day trading, but it does still carry risks. Let's look at the top mistakes made by new swing traders.

Failing to use a stop-loss

Always use a stop loss on your orders so that you minimize potential losses.

Risking too much on a trade

Remember to only risk 1-2% of the capital in your investment account on an individual trade.

Not being careful with leverage

Remember swing traders can use 2:1 leverage. If you're careless, this can get you into big financial trouble.

Letting yourself be driven by emotion

Many new traders get worked up with emotion watching securities move. During this experience, they can get impatient or find themselves fearing they will miss out on a big win. However, this leads to bad moves by the trader, selling too soon or throwing too much money after something they think is a sure thing that turns out to be a bust. Or maybe they enter the trade too early. Instead of being driven by emotions in the heat of the moment new traders need to stay focused on using the analysis and techniques described in this book and go into deeper research to learn more.

Unrealistic Expectations

Swing trading is not a get rich quick scheme. Many new traders have unrealistic expectations that they will become a millionaire overnight. Not only does it take time to become a successful trader and build wealth, but it takes an awful lot of hard work. To become a successful trader, you have to spend a lot of time studying the markets, paying attention to financial news, learning how to read charts, studying the companies and so on. None of this is easy, it takes work.

Giving in to panic

Panic can lead traders to sell and take losses or fail to realize gains they could have had. Again, this is an emotional response. Instead of fearing that you'll lose everything you should follow the suggested rules for risk and always use stop loss orders to minimize potential losses.

Greed

Staying in a trade too long in the hopes of getting rich quick has undone many new investors. A new trader should set profit goals for each trade and stick with them. Use OCO orders so that the order takes care of the profits as well as the losses for you so that you don't stay in a position too long and then miss out on profits, losing money instead as the stock price declines.

Getting arrogant after a few wins

In the event that you rack up a few successful trades, you might get cocky about it and become overconfident. But be aware, if you are not careful the bad trades will find you and the losses will come. Getting arrogant rather than maintaining a humble attitude which will lead you to carefully study the markets and taking precautions while shooting for realistic profits can lead to big trouble over the longer term.

Failing to Plan

Trading for the hell of it is not a plan. Neither is trading hoping that millions will come, so trading as if you are playing the lottery, this is not a good strategy to follow. You need to lay out a specific plan before you place your first trade. Have realistic goals and always know what your goals are. Once you meet the goals then you can readjust. Your goals should be modest in the beginning, that way they will be easier to meet. Set out ahead of time how much capital you are going to risk and what your specific goals for profit are going to be. When you meet your goals, don't blow it by losing focus. Set more realistic and attainable goals with reasonable levels of risk.

Failing to take time to learn

Congratulations! No, I mean that seriously. By reading this book, you have already shown that you are the kind of person who is willing to sit down and take the time to learn about the markets before diving in. However, there is a lot to learn about stocks, trading, and options. You should be constantly learning, reading as many books as possible, watching YouTube videos, and taking a training course. You may also benefit from personally getting to know other traders in your area to learn from them and trade experiences. The stock market is very complicated, and even seasoned veterans make large mistakes and lose a lot of money. You can never learn enough about it so be sure to keep putting in the time to improve your knowledge. When it comes to the stock market, trading, and options, you should consider yourself a lifelong learner.

Don't buy out of the money options

Out of the money options are cheap, however, remember that the probability of the stock moving enough to turn an out of the money option to one that is in the money is relatively low. An out of the money option is a bad way to invest.

Ignoring Time Value

Remember that the three things that impact the price of an option are whether it's in the money or out of the money, that is what the strike price is relative to the current stock price, volatility, and time value. Time value always decreases with each passing day, so you need to know where the option stands with respect to time value.

Buying options close to expiration

This is somewhat similar to buying options that are out of the money. As an option gets closer to expiration, they get cheaper. New traders think they are snapping up bargains by buying options that are close to expiration. However, the closer an option gets to expiration, the more worthless it becomes especially if it's out of the money. Buying an option that is both out of the money and close to expiration would be a really bad move.

Trade in the right time frames

Swing trading is a short-term activity, but it's not day trading. How long a time frame is involved depends on whom you ask. Many swing traders will be trading on a 2-6-day time frame. If that isn't comfortable for you, that's fine. You can always stretch it out further, even out to 100 days or so. But don't be so risk averse that you fail to exit your positions. If that becomes an issue maybe long-term investing is more your style. On the other hand, if you find that swing trading isn't exciting enough when you've put together enough capital to open an account (you are going to need $25,000 at a minimum) then maybe day trading is where you belong. The reality is that you are going to have more success trading at a level that is most comfortable for you. Don't swing trade because other people think day trading is too dangerous or do it because you're a long term investor who's getting mocked by their trading friends.

Tips for Success

Stay away from calls that are Out of the Money: If a call is not at least at the money then it is not worth your time. While you have likely heard the old adage, buy low and sell high, that is never the right choice in this case as calls that are out of the money are much less likely to get back to where they need to be if you hope to turn a profit on them. This, in turn, amounts to little more than gambling because there are always going to be relatively few indicators that you can rely on to determine if the price is going to stabilize in the time allotted.

It is important to keep in mind that buying an option means knowing what direction an underlying stock is going to move in, but it is just as important to know when it is going to move in that direction. If you misjudge either, then you are likely to lose out on the commission in addition to not being able to use that money in other more profitable ways until the option expires. Don't forget, in order to make money you need the option to increase all the way from out of the money to the strike price if you want to make a profit.

Work out multiple strategies: Eventually you will start to feel constrained by the system or plan that you are utilizing and want to expand into a wider variety of options. When this happens it is important that you work out new plans and strategies instead of trying to force your existing strategy to work in ways that it was not designed to. Certain strategies are always only going to work in certain scenarios and trying to force them to do otherwise is just asking for trouble. What's worse, these faulty decisions are going to taint your overall trade average, making your plan seem worse than it actually is.

Utilize a spread: A long spread is comprised of a pair of options, one with a higher cost and the other with a lower cost. The higher cost option is the one that you will buy and the other is the one that you will sell. Everything about the pair of options should be the same except for their strike prices. When using a spread, it is important that you always keep the time value in mind or else you will find yourself in a scenario where it serves to limit your profits.

Always be clear on when you will be entering or exiting: Ensuring that you know exactly when you want to start a trade or to exit an existing trade can become more difficult the more your emotions begin to come into play.

While it will be difficult to leave money on the table at first, having limits to your trade will keep you from losing much more money than it will ultimately cost you. What's more, when you think about the amount of money that you are likely to gain in the short period between when you should exit a trade and when you ultimately do, the amount saved is typically going to be negligible.

Don't double up: If a trade that appears as though it is going to turn a profit suddenly and unexpectedly moves in the wrong direction, the reaction of many novice options traders is going to be let emotion get the better of you and possibly double down on what is rapidly becoming a bad investment in hopes of making back all of the money that was previously lost. If you find yourself in a situation where you are thinking about doubling down on something questionable you can keep yourself from making the wrong decision by first asking yourself if you would have made the decision if things had gone your way from the start. In nearly all scenarios, cutting your losses and moving forward with a clear head is the preferable action. Remember, there are always more profitable trades on the horizon.

Keep earnings dates in mind: When it comes to maximizing your earnings potential it is important to have a clear idea of when any of the underlying stocks related to your options are going to have to disclose their earnings for the past quarter. Regardless of what the outcome of these calls is going to be, they are sure to generate a fair amount of movement when it comes to the stock in question which means being caught unaware can leave you trading based on information that is suddenly extremely outdated. Option prices typically tend to spike around earnings time as a result.

Additionally, it is important to keep in mind when any underlying stock is going to be paying dividends as well. This is extremely important because unless you exercise the options related to the stocks that are going to be paying dividends then you won't make any money in the process. These dividends can sometimes be assigned earlier than expected which is why you always want to have a firm grasp on the newest information available regarding the dates in question.

Understand the risk of early assignment: It is common for new traders to sell options or months without realizing they are putting themselves at risk until they are handed their first early assignment and are forced to deal with it in any way possible. The early assignment occurs when a holder exercises their rights well before the expiration date of the option in question that you are the writer on and it means you have to fulfill your obligation even if the terms aren't as much in your favor as you would like. If this happens to you the best thing you can do is not to let your emotions get the better of you and instead look for ways to make the best of a bad situation before committing to anything specific.

Commit to spreads only when appropriate: When you are first starting out it can be easy to start a spread, consider all available options and then setting up the remainder of the spread. If you typically find yourself buying a call, finding the best possible moment, and then setting up a sell call then you will likely find yourself in a situation where a sudden change of fortune between the two makes seeing even a marginal return on your investment more difficult than you previously intended. This can easily be presented by committing to a spread all at once as this will provide fewer chances for various variables to sneak in and ruin your calculations.

Trade what you can afford to lose: One of the most difficult lessons for many new options traders to learn is that you must never put more into a trade than you can realistically afford to lose, regardless of how good of a deal the trade appears to be at the time. There is never, ever going to be a trade that is a sure thing which means that luck will always play a factor no matter how airtight your system may have appeared to be in the past. If you typically take bigger risks than you can realistically afford, it isn't a question of if you will learn your lesson, it is a matter of when.

Conclusion

Options trading is a great way to enter the market with a small amount of capital. The premiums keep changing and you can make a lot of money if you trade wisely and do not take unnecessary risks.

This book has explained all the important facts about the options trade. It has tried to throw light on all the aspects of options trading so that you understand the functioning of the market. Trading is just a psychological game. Both parties are trying to guess the direction of the wind. The seller is taking a bigger risk but the profit of the seller is also sturdy as the seller is an experienced player. You have to understand the psyche of the seller.

Knowledge is power when it comes to trading. It is not a guessing game. You are speculating about the rates and the way the market will behave, yet you must have a plan and reasoning behind the actions. Once in the trade, this knowledge will help you in figuring the market will move and the kind of profits you can expect to make.

The biggest mistake new traders make is not calculating the real value hidden in the trade. A contract that may look attractive might not have any real value at all. You must pay special attention to that part.

The aim of this book is to explain the main concepts of options trading and how it works. You will have to form strategies to move into the market and you will definitely make a profit.

www.ingramcontent.com/pod-product-compliance
Lightning Source LLC
Chambersburg PA
CBHW070647220526
45466CB00001B/325